DECODABLE WORDS, SIGHT WORDS & SPELLING

Teacher Resources for Blended Learning

Vol. 1
Print Concepts & Phonological Awareness

Vol. 2
Letter Sounds

Vol. 3
Decodable Words, Sight Words & Spelling

Vol. 4
Reading Comprehension: Grades K-1

Vol. 5
Reading Comprehension: Grades 2-3

Vol. 6
Reading Comprehension: Grades 4+

Vol. 7
Grammar, Vocabulary, Speaking & Listening

Available at imaginelearning.com/bookstore

Developed and published by Imagine Learning, Inc.

September 2016 Edition

ISBN 978-1-945460-02-9

CONTENTS

DECODABLE WORDS

This section includes activities, resources, and lessons to help students learn to decode words and read texts independently.

Notes

Using Imagine Learning in the Classroom

Blended Learning with Imagine Learning

Along with the lessons and activities in this volume, Imagine Learning offers a wealth of digital instructional activities. Used together, the offline and online teaching materials provide teachers more flexibility to teach language and literacy within a blended learning environment.

Implementation Options

Offline lessons and online resources can be used for whole group lessons, small group interventions, or individual coaching sessions. Imagine Learning's individualized learning paths also allow students to learn independently at their own individual levels.

TEACHER-LED INSTRUCTION

Because Imagine Learning activities teach key language and literacy skills, teachers can select desired lessons for focused whole-class instruction, practice, and review. Projecting activities or using them with an interactive white board makes it easy for everyone to participate.

ONE-ON-ONE INSTRUCTION

Teachers can use the Action Areas Tool to gain insight on where individual students are struggling and use that information to provide focused instruction. This data is especially helpful as you create an RTI plan and work on skills remediation. Teachers can also extend learning by reviewing student recordings and written responses to offer direct feedback.

SMALL-GROUP INSTRUCTION

The Action Areas Tool pinpoints where groups of students are struggling and immediately creates skill-based intervention groups. The tool also suggests online activities and reteaching lessons that allow for targeted intervention.

COMPUTER BANK OR LAB ROTATION

Imagine Learning provides each student with an individualized learning path by providing systematic, adaptive instruction. This makes it ideal for independent student learning—whether it be at an in-class station or in a computer lab.

Digital Imagine Learning Activities

Teachers can access Imagine Learning's engaging digital activities through the Activity Menu. The Activity Menu is organized by curriculum area. For digital activities that match the skills in this volume, click the corresponding curriculum area. Use the functions below to find the best settings for your class.

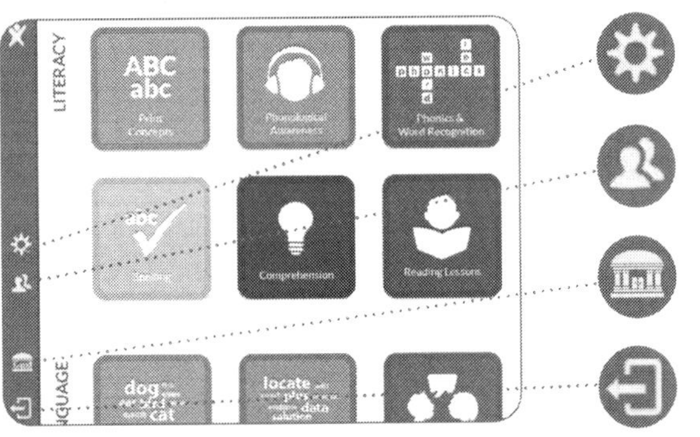

Change **program settings,** including first-language support.

Launch the **Imagine Learning Portal** to find reports, management functions, and additional resources.

Enter the **Imagine Museum** to preview performance-based student engagement features.

Log out of the Activity Menu and return to the **login page.**

Reports and Tools

Tools for setting up the program and monitoring student progress and growth are provided to teachers and administrators. Reviewing data regularly, as well as analyzing student recordings and writings, drives program efficacy and success.

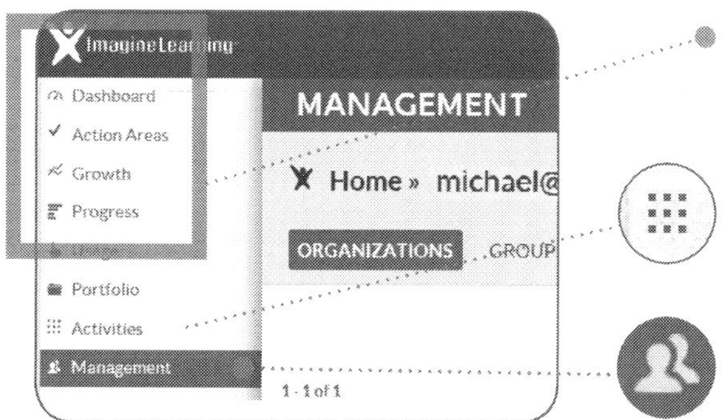

Review group and individual student data, and listen to student recordings.

Launch Activity Menu and Teacher Resources.

Manage classroom and student account preferences (session time, student passwords, etc.).

Action Areas Tool

Use data from the Action Areas Tool to identify individual students or groups of students that struggle with a particular skill. Action Areas will also suggest online activities that can be used to help struggling students.

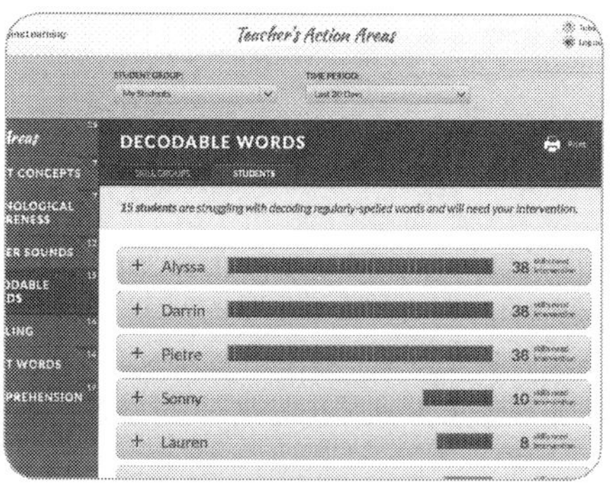

The left navigation pane lists all curriculum areas.

This number denotes how many students are struggling in a curriculum area.

Click a curriculum area and click **Intervention Tools** to view details, suggested activities, and printouts.

Teacher Resources

All Classroom Activities and Reteaching Lessons included in this volume can also be found in the Teacher Resources section online.

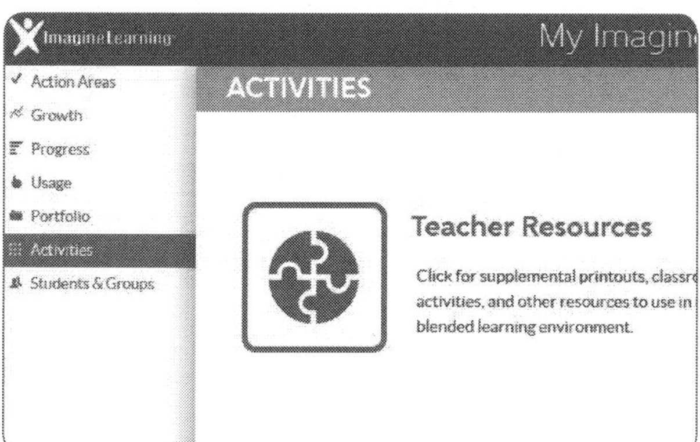

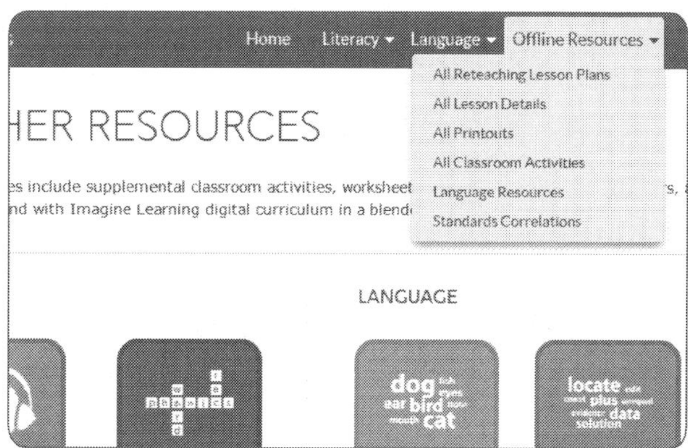

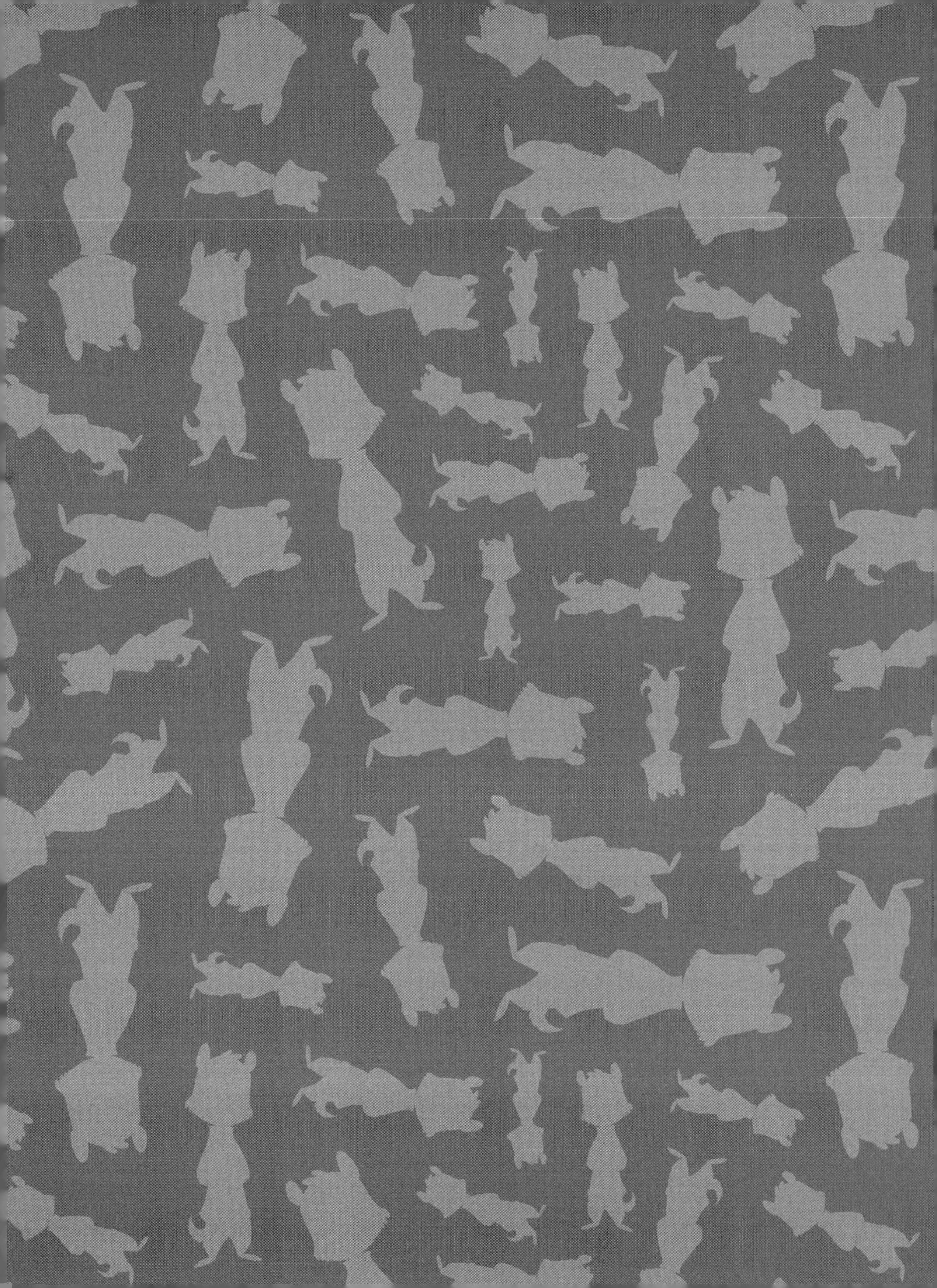

DECODABLE WORDS

CLASSROOM ACTIVITIES

Classroom activities include lesson plans and resources for whole-class activities that help students develop decoding skills. The interactive and engaging methods of instruction and practice reinforce the skills students learn from the Imagine Learning online curriculum and provide opportunities for students to actively demonstrate knowledge. These standards-based activities can be used for a variety of instructional needs and settings.

- Hands-on activities to practice and reinforce decoding skills
- Standards-based materials that require minimal teacher preparation

Blend It Together

CCSS.RF.1.3.B
TEKS 110.12.3.A

LEARNING OBJECTIVE: Blend onsets and rimes to decode short vowel words.
LANGUAGE OBJECTIVE: Read short vowel words by blending onsets and rimes.

Activity Overview

Students put onset and rime flashcards together to decode short vowel words.

Materials	Preparation
• Onset-Rime Flash Cards	• Prepare onset-rime flashcards.

Explain

Introduce the activity: ***We can put these beginning sounds together with these endings to make words.***

Play

1. Select an onset card and a rime card.
2. Have two students come to the front of the class to hold up the cards.
3. Point to the onset card and say the sound. Ask students to say it with you.
4. Point to the rime card and say the rime. Ask students to say it with you.
5. Invite students to put the two sets of sounds together.
6. Have the class say the word without a break between the onset and rime; for example, if students hear */k/... /an/*, they should blend the sounds together and say, "can."
7. Use the word in context. Use the sentence provided or create a new sentence of your own.
8. Repeat the activity with other onsets and rimes.

Onsets	Rimes	Words	Sentences
/h/ /b/ /f/ /s/ /p/	/at/	hat bat fat sat pat	He put his **hat** on his head. The boy hit the ball with his **bat**. The dog was round and **fat**. She **sat** on the chair and watched TV. **Pat** the puppy on his head.
/r/ /b/ /t/	/ag/	rag bag tag	Take the **rag** and wipe off the table. Put the toys inside the **bag**. A **tag** shows how much a toy costs.
/h/ /t/ /k/	/op/	hop top cop	The rabbit will **hop** across the yard. The **top** of the hill is covered in snow. The **cop** stood on the corner.
/h/ /p/ /d/ /g/ /l/	/ot/	hot pot dot got lot	The stove is **hot**. Put the **pot** on the stove. A period looks like a **dot**. She **got** the doll. A room full of people is a **lot**.
/b/ /f/ /h/ /p/ /s/	/it/	bit fit hit pit sit	The boy **bit** the apple. The pants are too tight and don't **fit**. **Hit** the ball hard and it will go far. The **pit** was deep in the ground. I **sit** on the bench.
/f/ /s/ /r/	/un/	fun sun run	Playing all day long is **fun**. The **sun** is bright and hot. He can **run** very fast.
/k/ /f/ /m/ /p/ /r/ /t/	/an/	can fan man pan ran tan	He **can** go outside to play. The **fan** blew air into his face. The **man** was her father. The **pan** was full of water. The horse **ran** around the pasture. The dog is not dark brown but **tan**.

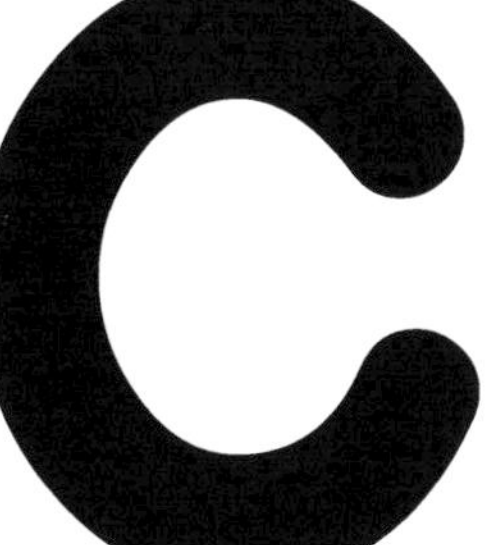

g

h

l

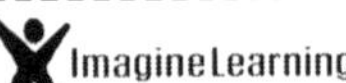

p

s

at

ag

op

it

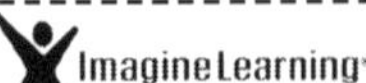

un

an

ot

Classroom Activities

Word Factory

CCSS.RF.1.3.B
TEKS 110.12.3.A

LEARNING OBJECTIVE: Build and decode CVC words.
LANGUAGE OBJECTIVE: Use phonics knowledge to sound out and say short vowel words.

Activity Overview

Students work in groups to make and read CVC words using letter cards.

Materials	Preparation
• Letter Cards, uppercase or lowercase (1 set per group)	• Cut out Letter Cards.

Explain

Display a set of letter cards. Say: ***Let's use these letter cards to make words with short vowels.***

Model the activity: ***First I choose a vowel:*** a, ***/a/. Then I choose a letter for the beginning of the word:*** c, ***/k/. And then I will choose a letter for the end of the word:*** p, ***/p/. When I put them all together, what is the word? That's right, the word is*** cap.

Divide students into groups of three and distribute the letter card sets. Say: ***Let's do one word together. The word is*** mop. ***One person in your group will start the word with the vowel: the letter*** o. ***Now the next person will find the letter*** m ***and put it in front of*** o ***to make the beginning of the word. Then the next person will find the letter*** p ***and put it at the end of the word. What word have we made?*** (mop) Have the students repeat the word.

Continue: ***Now you will work with your group to make more words. For each word, one person in your group will choose the vowel:*** a, e, i, o, ***or*** u. ***Then one person will choose the letter for the beginning, and one person will choose a letter for the end of the word. I will give you about 15 seconds to make your first word. Then each group will hold up their word and we will read it together as a class.***

Play

1. Have students work in groups of three to create a word.
2. Remind students to choose the vowel first, then the beginning letter, then the ending letter.
3. Signal to indicate time is up. (Adjust 15-second time limit as needed.)
4. Have each group stand, one at a time, and display their letters in the correct order to form a word. Each student should hold one letter.
5. Have each student say the letter sound he or she are holding.
6. Have the class read the word aloud chorally.

EXTENSION ACTIVITY: Make extra copies of common consonants to provide more options for students. Prompt students with knowledge of blends and digraphs to use those patterns to create CVCC and CCVC words.

C

D

E

F

G

H

I

J

K

L

M

O

P

Q

R

S

T

W

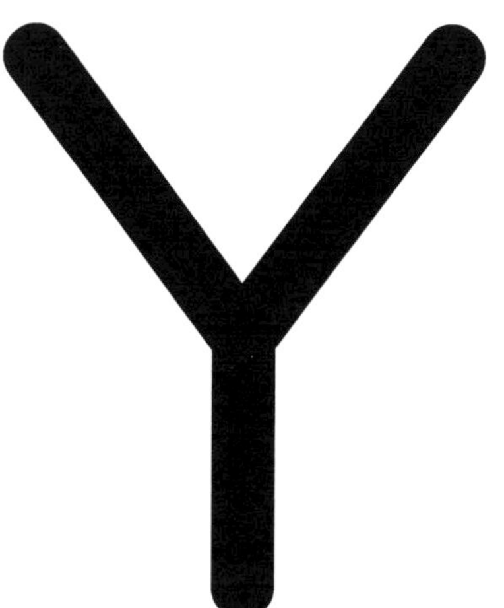

a

b

c

d

e

f	g
h	i
j	

Classroom Activities

m

n

o

p

q

r

s

t

u

v

w

x

y

z

Notes

Classroom Activities

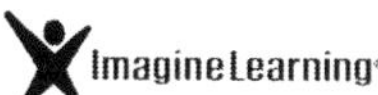

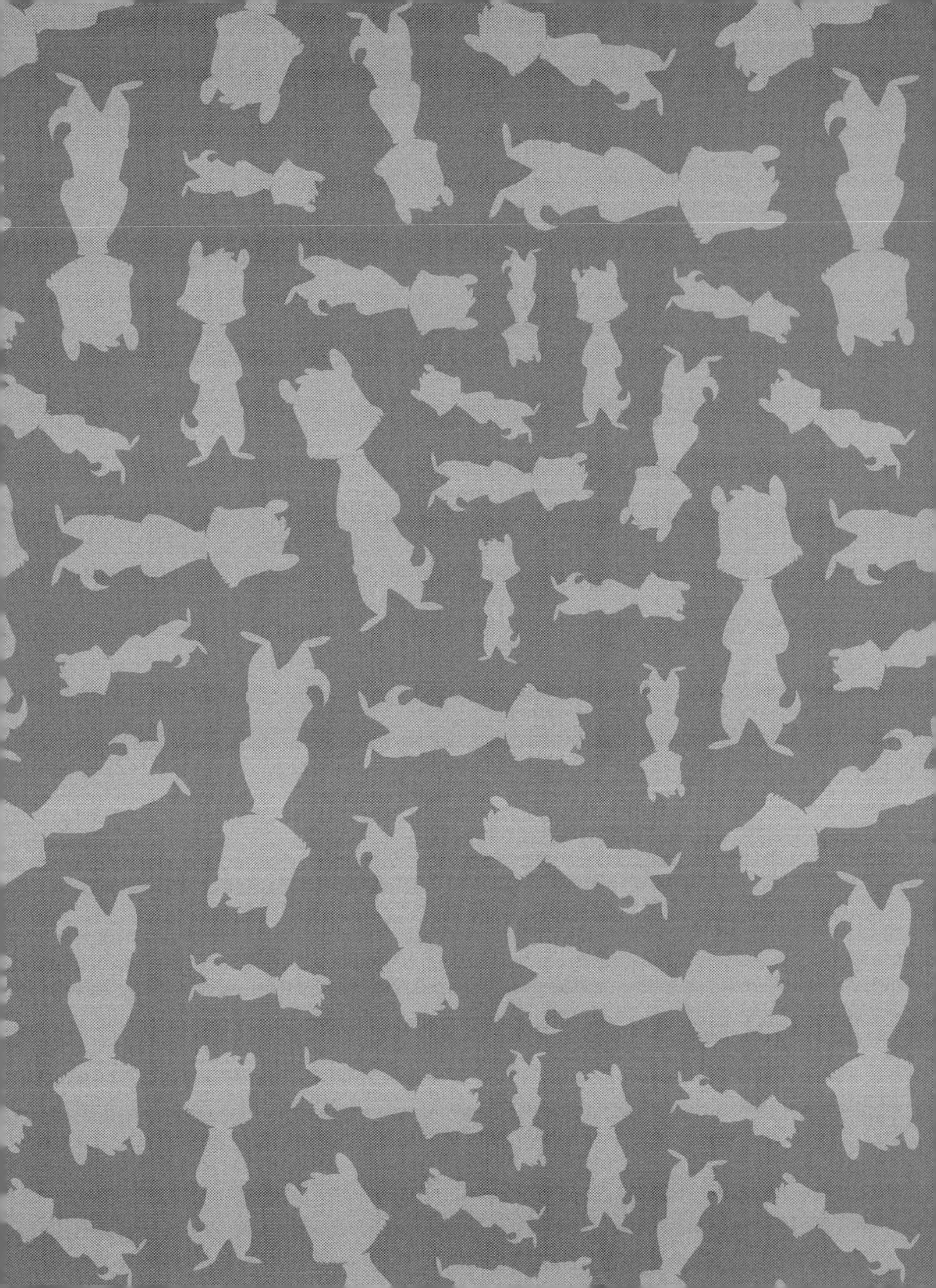

DECODABLE WORDS

RETEACHING LESSONS

Developed with research-based methods, these lessons provide additional instruction to help students decode word parts in single-syllable and multisyllable words, learn vowel team conventions, read words with common affixes and beginning and ending letter combinations, and read words by analogy in context. Each 10–20-minute lesson plan can be used for small group intervention or skill review.

Analyze data in the Imagine Learning Action Areas Tool to identify groups of students who struggle with decodable words, and use the Reteaching Lessons as a tool to support those students.

- Complete lesson plans that include modeling, practice, and assessment
- A variety of multi-sensory strategies in an easy-to-follow format
- Game cards, letter tiles, printouts, and decodable sentences and texts
- Grab-and-go, easy-prep lessons specifically designed for struggling learners

Progress Tracking Sheet

Date	Student Name	Lesson/Skill	Intervention Successful (Y/N)	Notes

Progress Tracking Sheet

Date	Student Name	Lesson/Skill	Intervention Successful (Y/N)	Notes

Reteaching Lessons

Notes

Word Building with /ă/

Grade 1

10 min.

CCSS.RF.K.3b
TEKS 110.11.3.B

LEARNING OBJECTIVE: Decode words using the short *a* sound (/ă/) in a CVC word.
LANGUAGE OBJECTIVE: Use phonics clues to sound out and read words with the short *a* sound.

Lesson Overview

Students use letter tiles to build new words by replacing one letter at a time. Students then blend sounds of letters to read the new words.

Materials	Preparation
• Pocket chart • Large Letter Cards m, a, t, p • Build a Word printout (one for each student) • *Do Not Tap* decodable text (one for each student pair) • Word Stairs printout (extension activity)	• Cut out Large Letter Cards. • Cut out the letter tiles *a*, *m*, *d*, *s*, *t*, and *p* from each Build a Word printout.

Teach and Model

Display pocket chart. Hold up large letter cards.

Say: ***Let's use letters you have learned to build some words.***

Model word building: ***I will build the first word,* mat. *The first sound in* mat *is* /m/. *What letter stands for* /m/?** Place the letter card *m* in the pocket chart.

Say: ***The middle sound is /ă/. What letter stands for /ă/?*** Place the letter *a* in the pocket chart.

Say: ***The last sound is /t/. What letter stands for /t/?*** Place the letter *t* in the pocket chart.

Say: ***Now let's read the whole word:* mat.** As students say *mat*, sweep your finger under the word.

Model: ***Watch as I change just one letter in this word to make a new word.*** Replace the letter card *m* with the letter card *p*.

Ask: ***What is the sound for* p*? What is the new word?*** As students say *pat*, sweep your finger under the word.

Practice and Apply

Give each student a copy of the Build a Word printout and a set of letter tiles (*a*, *m*, *d*, *s*, *t*, *p*). Instruct students to say the name of each letter tile and place it in the builder box. Then have students build the model word *pat* by sliding letters up from the builder box and along the arrow.

Say: ***Let's build a new word.*** Take *p* from *pat* and replace it with *s*.

Ask: ***What is the new word?***

Have students sweep their finger under the word *sat* and say it together. Write the word in a column on the board.

Say: ***Now change* t *to* p. *What's the new word?***

Have students sweep their finger under the word *sap* and say it together. Add the word to the column on the board.

Continue the process with the following letters and words:

- change *s* to *t* (*tap*)
- change *t* to *m* (*map*)
- change *p* to *d* (*mad*)
- change *m* to *s* (*sad*)

Say: ***Now I'll tell you the new word, and you change one letter to make it.***

- *pad* (change *s* to *p*)
- *pam* (change *d* to *m*)
- *pat* (change *m* to *t*)
- *sat* (change *p* to *s*)
- *mat* (change *s* to *m*)

Have students read the column of words on the board

Practice and Apply

Divide students into pairs. Give each student pair a copy of *Do Not Tap*.

Explain: ***The name of this story is* Do Not Tap. *Practice reading it with your partner. Take turns reading one line at a time. When you are the listener, remember to read along silently and point to each word as your partner reads. If your partner makes a mistake, help your partner by saying the correct word.*** Allow students time to read the story. Listen to each pair of students read.

*Do Not Tap**

Tap, **tap**, **tap**.
"What is **that**?"
Pat, **pat**, **pat**.
"**Mat**, what is **that**?"
Tap, **tap**, **tap**.
"Do not **tap**, **Pam**."
Pat, **pat**, **pat**.
"Do not **pat**, **Mat**."
"Do not **tap** or **pat**."
"Now we can **tap** and **pat**."
"I'm good, **Mat**."
"I'm good, **Pam**."
*/ă/ CVC words are identified in bold

Check Progress

Observe student during practice activities and use the following assessment to determine student's success on the target skill. If the student can correctly read two words, consider the intervention successful.

Build a CVC word using the large letter cards. Have a student read it aloud. Continue with the words in the word bank, repeating words when necessary, until each student has successfully read two words.

CVC word bank: pad, pat, mad, mat, map, dam, sad, sat, sap, tad, tap

Extension Activity

Give each student a copy of the Word Stairs printout and a set of letter tiles (*a*, *m*, *d*, *p*, *s*, *t*) from the bottom of the Build a Word printout. Give students these instructions and then observe them as they work independently.

1. ***Select three letter tiles to make a real word.***
2. ***Read the word out loud and write the word on the first step.***
3. ***Make a new word with the letter tiles.***
4. ***Read the new word out loud and write the word on the next step.***
5. ***Continue until all the steps are filled.***

If time allows, invite volunteers to talk about two of their words.

Ask: ***How are the words alike? How are they different?***

Reteaching Lessons

m

a

t

p

Build a Word

a	m	d	s	t	p

Reteaching Lessons

Name: ________________________________

Do Not Tap

Tap, tap, tap

"What is that?

Pat, pat, pat.

"Mat, what is that?"

Tap, tap, tap

"Do not tap, Pam."

Pat, pat, pat.

"Do not pat, Mat."

"Do not tap or pat."

"Now we can tap and pat."

"I'm good, Mat."

"I'm good, Pam."

Reteaching Lessons

Name: ____________________

Word Stairs

Reteaching Lessons

Word Building with /ĕ/

Grade 1

10 min.

CCSS.RF.K.3b
TEKS 110.11.3.B

LEARNING OBJECTIVE: Decode words using the short *e* sound (/ĕ/) in a CVC word.

LANGUAGE OBJECTIVE: Use phonics clues to sound out and read words with the short *e* sound.

Lesson Overview

Students use letter tiles to build new words by replacing one letter at a time. Students then blend sounds of letters to read the new words.

Materials	Preparation
• Pocket chart • Large Letter Cards t, e, n, m • Build a Word printout (one for each student) • *Ten Hens* decodable text (one for each student pair) • Word Stairs printout (extension activity)	• Cut out Large Letter Cards. • Cut out the letter tiles *e, i, m, p, d, t, l, b, r, n,* and *g* from each Build a Word printout.

Teach and Model

Display pocket chart. Hold up the large letter cards.

Say: ***Let's use letters you have learned to build some words.***

Model word building: ***I will build the first word,* ten. *The first sound in* ten *is /t/. What letter stands for /t/?*** Place the letter card *t* in the pocket chart.

Say: ***The middle sound is /ĕ/. What letter stands for /ĕ/?*** Place the letter *e* in the pocket chart.

Say: ***The last sound is /n/. What letter stands for /n/?*** Place the letter *n* in the pocket chart.

Say: ***Now let's read the whole word:* ten.** As students say *ten*, sweep your finger under the word.

Model: ***Watch as I change just one letter in this word to make a new word.*** Replace the letter card *t* with the letter card *m*.

Ask: ***What is the sound for* m*? What is the new word?*** As students say *men*, sweep your finger under the word.

Practice and Apply

Give each student a copy of the Build a Word printout and a set of letter tiles (*e, i, m, p, d, t, l, b, r, n, g*). Instruct students to say the name of each letter tile and place it in the builder box. Then have students build the model word *men* by sliding letters up from the builder box and along the arrow.

Say: ***Let's build a new word.*** Take *n* from *men* and replace it with *t*.

Ask: ***What is the new word?***

Have students sweep their finger under the word *met* and say it together. Write the word in a column on the board.

Say: ***Now change* m *to* n*. What's the new word?***

Have students sweep their finger under the word *net* and say it together. Add the word to the column on the board.

Continue the process with the following letters and words:

- change *n* to *l* (*let*)
- change *l* to *p* (*pet*)
- change *e* to *i* (*pit*)
- change *t* to *n* (*pin*)
- change *n* to *g* (*pig*)
- change *i* to *e* (*peg*)

Say: ***Now I'll tell you the new word, and you change one letter to make it.***

- *leg* (change *p* to *l*)
- *led* (change *g* to *d*)
- *bed* (change *l* to *b*)
- *bid* (change *e* to *i*)
- *rid* (change *b* to *r*)
- *red* (change *i* to *e*)

Have students read the column of words on the board

Practice and Apply

Divide students into pairs. Give each student pair a copy of *Ten Hens.*

Explain: ***The name of this story is* Ten Hens. *Practice reading it with your partner. Take turns reading one line at a time. When you are the listener, remember to read along silently and point to each word as your partner reads. If your partner makes a mistake, help your partner by saying the correct word.*** Allow students time to read the story. Listen to each pair of students read.

*Ten Hens**

Jen has **ten hens**.
Ten big, **red hens**.
The **hens** are in the **pen**.
Good job, **hens**.
Jen can **get** the **eggs**.
Jen sets the **eggs** in a bin.
Look, **ten eggs**!
Ten eggs with tan **shells**.
Good job, **hens**.
Jen lets her **hens** go to bed.
Jen **sets** the **eggs** in a pan.
Here are the **ten eggs**.
Good job, **hens**.
Good job, **Jen**!

*/ĕ/ CVC words are identified in bold

Reteaching Lessons

Check Progress

Observe student during practice activities and use the following assessment to determine student's success on the target skill. If the student can correctly read two words, consider the intervention successful.

Build a CVC word using the large letter cards. Have a student read it aloud. Continue with the words in the word bank, repeating words when necessary, until each student has successfully read two words.

CVC word bank: beg, fed, get, let, pen, set, yet, hem, hen, den, jet, pet

Extension Activity

Give each student a copy of the Word Stairs printout and a set of letter tiles (*e, i, m, p, d, t, l, b, r, n, g*) from the bottom of the Build a Word printout. Give students these instructions and then observe them as they work independently.

1. ***Select three letter tiles to make a real word.***
2. ***Read the word out loud and write the word on the first step.***
3. ***Make a new word with the letter tiles.***
4. ***Read the new word out loud and write the word on the next step.***
5. ***Continue until all the steps are filled.***

If time allows, invite volunteers to talk about two of their words.

Ask: ***How are the words alike? How are they different?***

t

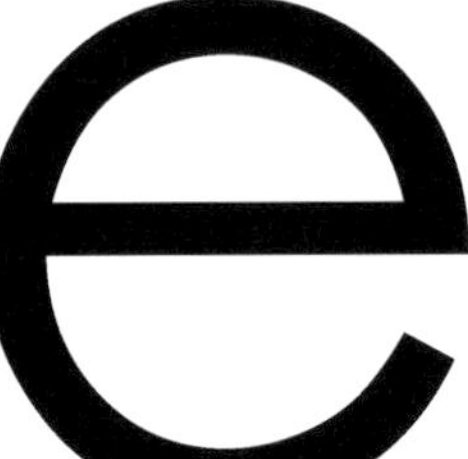
e

n

m

Build a Word

e	i	m	p	d	t
l	b	r	n	g	

Reteaching Lessons ✓

Name: ______________________________

Ten Hens

Jen has ten hens.
Ten big red hens.
The hens are in the pen.
Good job, hens.

Jen can get the eggs.
Jen sets the eggs in a bin.
Look, ten eggs!
Ten eggs with tan shells.
Good job, hens.

Jen lets her hens go to bed.
Jen sets the eggs in a pan.

Here are the ten eggs.
Good job, hens.
Good job, Jen!

Name: ____________________

Word Stairs

Reteaching Lessons

Word Building with /ĭ/

LEARNING OBJECTIVE: Decode words using the short *i* sound (/ĭ/) in a CVC word.
LANGUAGE OBJECTIVE: Use phonics clues to sound out and read words with the short *i* sound.

Lesson Overview

Students use letter tiles to build new words by replacing one letter at a time. Students then blend sounds of letters to read the new words.

Materials	Preparation
• Pocket chart • Large Letter Cards h, i, d, b • Build a Word printout (one for each student) • *Pip Can Fix It* decodable text (one for each student pair) • Word Stairs printout (extension activity)	• Cut out Large Letter Cards. • Cut out the letter tiles *a, i, h, b, p, t, d, n,* and *s* from each Build a Word printout.

Teach and Model

Display pocket chart. Hold up the large letter cards.

Say: ***Let's use letters you have learned to build some words.***

Model word building: ***I will build the first word,* hid. *The first sound in* hid *is* /h/. *What letter stands for* /h/?** Place the letter card *h* in the pocket chart.

Say: ***The middle sound is* /ĭ/. *What letter stands for* /ĭ/?** Place the letter *i* in the pocket chart.

Say: ***The last sound is* /d/. *What letter stands for* /d/?** Place the letter *d* in the pocket chart.

Say: ***Now let's read the whole word:* hid.** As students say *hid*, sweep your finger under the word.

Model: ***Watch as I change just one letter in this word to make a new word.*** Replace the letter card *h* with the letter card *b*.

Ask: ***What is the sound for* b? *What is the new word?*** As students say *bid*, sweep your finger under the word.

Practice and Apply

Give each student a copy of the Build a Word printout and a set of letter tiles (*a, i, h, b, p, t, d, n, s*). Instruct students to say the name of each letter tile and place it in the builder box. Then have students build the model word *men* by sliding letters up from the builder box and along the arrow.

Say: ***Let's build a new word.*** Take *d* from *bid* and replace it with *n*.

Ask: ***What is the new word?***

Have students sweep their finger under the word *bin* and say it together. Write the word in a column on the board.

Say: ***Now change* b *to* p. *What's the new word?***

Have students sweep their finger under the word *pin* and say it together. Add the word to the column on the board.

Continue the process with the following letters and words:

- change *i* to *a* (*pan*)
- change *p* to *t* (*tan*)
- change *a* to *i* (*tin*)
- change *n* to *p* (*tip*)
- change *i* to *a* (*tap*)
- change *t* to *n* (*nap*)
- change *a* to *i* (*nip*)

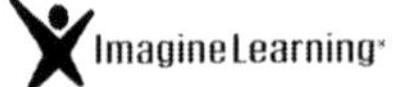

Say: ***Now I'll tell you the new word, and you change one letter to make it.***

- *sip* (change *n* to *s*)
- *sit* (change *p* to *t*)
- *hit* (change *s* to *h*)
- *bit* (change *h* to *b*)
- *bat* (change *i* to *a*)
- *pat* (change *b* to *p*)
- *pit* (change *a* to *i*)

Have students read the column of words on the board

Practice and Apply

Divide students into pairs. Give each student pair a copy of *Pip Can Fix It*.

Explain: ***The name of this story is* Pip Can Fix It. *Practice reading it with your partner. Take turns reading one line at a time. When you are the listener, remember to read along silently and point to each word as your partner reads. If your partner makes a mistake, help your partner by saying the correct word.*** Allow students time to read the story. Listen to each pair of students read.

*Pip Can Fix It**

Rim is big.
Rim likes to **dig**.
Oh no! "Stop, **Rim**!"
What can we do?
That's not so bad.
Pip can **fix** it.
Pip likes to **fix**.
Pip can **dig**.
Pip can **mix** and **dip**.
Here it is! It's like new.
"Be good, **Rim**. **Sit**!"
"Do not **dig**."
*/ĭ/ CVC words are identified in bold

Check Progress

Observe student during practice activities and use the following assessment to determine student's success on the target skill. If the student can correctly read two words, consider the intervention successful.

Build a CVC word using the large letter cards. Have a student read it aloud. Continue with the words in the word bank, repeating words when necessary, until each student has successfully read two words.

CVC word bank: bib, hip, dip, din, hit, nit, did, pin, tip, hid, bin, nip

Extension Activity

Give each student a copy of the Word Stairs printout and a set of letter tiles (*a*, *i*, *h*, *b*, *p*, *t*, *d*, *n*, *s*) from the bottom of the Build a Word printout. Give students these instructions and then observe them as they work independently.

1. ***Select three letter tiles to make a real word.***
2. ***Read the word out loud and write the word on the first step.***
3. ***Make a new word with the letter tiles.***
4. ***Read the new word out loud and write the word on the next step.***
5. ***Continue until all the steps are filled.***

If time allows, invite volunteers to talk about two of their words.

Ask: ***How are the words alike? How are they different?***

Reteaching Lessons

h

i

d

b

Reteaching Lessons

Name: ______________________________

Pip Can Fix It

Rim is big.

Rim likes to dig.

Oh no! "Stop, Rim!"

What can we do?

That's not so bad.

Pip can fix it.

Pip likes to fix.

Pip can dig.

Pip can mix and dip.

Here it is! It's like new.

"Be good, Rim. Sit!"

"Do not dig."

Reteaching Lessons

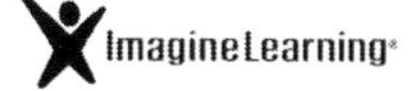

Build a Word

a	i	h	b	p	t
d	n	s			

✓ Reteaching Lessons

Name: ______________________

Word Stairs

Reteaching Lessons

Decodable Words

Word Building with /ŏ/

Grade 1

10 min.

CCSS.RF.K.3b
TEKS 110.11.3.B

LEARNING OBJECTIVE: Decode words using the short *o* sound (/ŏ/) in a CVC word.

LANGUAGE OBJECTIVE: Use phonics clues to sound out and read words with the short *o* sound.

Lesson Overview

Students use letter tiles to build new words by replacing one letter at a time. Students then blend sounds of letters to read the new words.

Materials	Preparation
• Pocket chart • Large Letter Cards h, o, t, p • Build a Word printout (one for each student) • *Stop, Bob, Stop* decodable text (one for each student pair) • Word Stairs printout (extension activity)	• Cut out Large Letter Cards. • Cut out the letter tiles *o, a, h, t, m, c, p, d,* and *n* from each Build a Word printout.

Teach and Model

Display pocket chart. Hold up the large letter cards.

Say: ***Let's use letters you have learned to build some words.***

Model word building: ***I will build the first word,* hot. *The first sound in* hot *is* /h/. *What letter stands for* /h/?** Place the letter card *h* in the pocket chart.

Say: ***The middle sound is /ŏ/. What letter stands for /ŏ/?*** Place the letter *o* in the pocket chart.

Say: ***The last sound is /t/. What letter stands for /t/?*** Place the letter *t* in the pocket chart.

Say: ***Now let's read the whole word:* hot.** As students say *hot*, sweep your finger under the word.

Model: ***Watch as I change just one letter in this word to make a new word.*** Replace the letter card *t* with the letter card *p*.

Ask: ***What is the sound for* p*? What is the new word?*** As students say *hop*, sweep your finger under the word.

Practice and Apply

Give each student a copy of the Build a Word printout and a set of letter tiles (*o, a, h, t, m, c, p, d, n*). Instruct students to say the name of each letter tile and place it in the builder box. Then have students build the model word *men* by sliding letters up from the builder box and along the arrow.

Say: ***Let's build a new word.*** Take *h* from *hop* and replace it with *t*.

Ask: ***What is the new word?***

Have students sweep their finger under the word *top* and say it together. Write the word in a column on the board.

Say: ***Now change* t *to* m. *What's the new word?***

Have students sweep their finger under the word *mop* and say it together. Add the word to the column on the board.

Continue the process with the following letters and words:

- change *o* to *a* (*map*)
- change *m* to *c* (*cap*)
- change *a* to *o* (*cop*)
- change *p* to *n* (*con*)
- change *n* to *t* (*cot*)

✓ Reteaching Lessons

- change *o* to *a* (*cat*)
- change *c* to *h* (*hat*)

Say: ***Now I'll tell you the new word, and you change one letter to make it.***

- *hot* (change *a* to *o*)
- *dot* (change *h* to *d*)
- *pot* (change *d* to *p*)
- *pat* (change *o* to *a*)
- *pad* (change *t* to *d*)
- *pod* (change *a* to *o*)
- *nod* (change *p* to *n*)

Have students read the column of words on the board

Practice and Apply

Divide students into pairs. Give each student pair a copy of *Stop, Bob, Stop.*

Explain: ***The name of this story is* Stop, Bob, Stop. *Practice reading it with your partner. Take turns reading one line at a time. When you are the listener, remember to read along silently and point to each word as your partner reads. If your partner makes a mistake, help your partner by saying the correct word.*** Allow students time to read the story. Listen to each pair of students read.

*Stop, Bob, Stop**

Mat is mad.
"**Stop**, **Bob**. That is bad!"
"**Stop**, **Tom**. That is bad!"
"No, no, **Bob**."
"No, no, **Tom**."
Mat is mad.
Bob is sad.
Tom is sad.
Then Mat is sad, too.
Mat pats **Bob** and **Tom**.
Mat is **not** mad.

*/ŏ/ CVC words are identified in bold

Check Progress

Observe student during practice activities and use the following assessment to determine student's success on the target skill. If the student can correctly read two words, consider the intervention successful.

Build a CVC word using the large letter cards. Have a student read it aloud. Continue with the words in the word bank, repeating words when necessary, until each student has successfully read two words.

CVC word bank: bot, not, pop, non, sob, hob, con, lot, lop, top, pod, cot

Extension Activity

Give each student a copy of the Word Stairs printout and a set of letter tiles (*o, a, h, t, m, c, p, d, n*) from the bottom of the Build a Word printout. Give students these instructions and then observe them as they work independently.

1. ***Select three letter tiles to make a real word.***
2. ***Read the word out loud and write the word on the first step.***
3. ***Make a new word with the letter tiles.***
4. ***Read the new word out loud and write the word on the next step.***
5. ***Continue until all the steps are filled.***

If time allows, invite volunteers to talk about two of their words.

Ask: ***How are the words alike? How are they different?***

Reteaching Lessons

Reteaching Lessons

h

o

t

p

Build a Word

o	a	h	t	m	c
p	d	n			

Reteaching Lessons

Name: ____________________

Stop, Bob, Stop

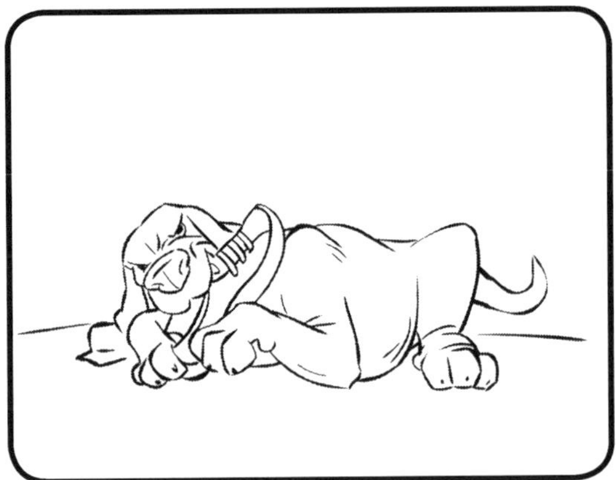

Mat is mad.

"Stop, Bob. That is bad!"

"Stop, Tom. That is bad!"

"No, no, Bob."

"No, no, Tom."

Mat is mad.

Bob is sad.

Tom is sad.

Then Mat is sad, too.

Mat pats Bob and Tom.

Mat is not mad.

Name: ______________________

Word Stairs

Decodable Words

Word Building with /ŭ/

Grade 1

10 min.

CCSS.RF.K.3b
TEKS 110.11.3.B

LEARNING OBJECTIVE: Decode words using the short *u* sound (/ŭ/) in a CVC word.

LANGUAGE OBJECTIVE: Use phonics clues to sound out and read words with the short *u* sound.

Lesson Overview

Students use letter tiles to build new words by replacing one letter at a time. Students then blend sounds of letters to read the new words.

Materials	Preparation
• Pocket chart • Large Letter Cards s, u, m, n • Build a Word printout (one for each student) • *Gus and I* decodable text (one for each student pair) • Word Stairs printout (extension activity)	• Cut out Large Letter Cards. • Cut out the letter tiles *a, u, r, s, b, h, n, g, t,* and *m* from each Build a Word printout.

Teach and Model

Display pocket chart. Hold up the large letter cards.

Say: ***Let's use letters you have learned to build some words.***

Model word building: ***I will build the first word,* sum. *The first sound in* sum *is /s/. What letter stands for /s/?*** Place the letter card *s* in the pocket chart.

Say: ***The middle sound is /ŭ/. What letter stands for /ŭ/?*** Place the letter *u* in the pocket chart.

Say: ***The last sound is /m/. What letter stands for /m/?*** Place the letter *t* in the pocket chart.

Say: ***Now let's read the whole word:* sum.** As students say *sum*, sweep your finger under the word.

Model: ***Watch as I change just one letter in this word to make a new word.*** Replace the letter card *m* with the letter card *n*.

Ask: ***What is the sound for* n*? What is the new word?*** As students say *sun*, sweep your finger under the word.

Reteaching Lessons

Practice and Apply

Give each student a copy of the Build a Word printout and a set of letter tiles (*a, u, r, s, b, h, n, g, t, m*). Instruct students to say the name of each letter tile and place it in the builder box. Then have students build the model word *men* by sliding letters up from the builder box and along the arrow.

Say: ***Let's build a new word.*** Take *s* from *sun* and replace it with *b*.

Ask: ***What is the new word?***

Have students sweep their finger under the word *bun* and say it together. Write the word in a column on the board.

Say: ***Now change* n *to* s. *What's the new word?***

Have students sweep their finger under the word *bus* and say it together. Add the word to the column on the board.

Continue the process with the following letters and words:

- change *s* to *g* (*bug*)
- change *u* to *a* (*bag*)
- change *b* to *h* (*hag*)
- change *a* to *u* (*hug*)
- change *h* to *r* (*rug*)
- change *u* to *a* (*rag*)
- change *g* to *n* (*ran*)

Say: ***Now I'll tell you the new word, and you change one letter to make it.***

- *run* (change *a* to *u*)
- *rut* (change *n* to *t*)
- *hut* (change *r* to *h*)
- *hat* (change *u* to *a*)
- *ham* (change *t* to *m*)
- *hum* (change *a* to *u*)
- *gum* (change *h* to *g*)

Have students read the column of words on the board

Practice and Apply

Divide students into pairs. Give each student pair a copy of *Gus and I*.

Explain: ***The name of this story is* Gus and I. *Practice reading it with your partner. Take turns reading one line at a time. When you are the listener, remember to read along silently and point to each word as your partner reads. If your partner makes a mistake, help your partner by saying the correct word.*** Allow students time to read the story. Listen to each pair of students read.

Gus and I*

We want to have **fun**,
My **pup**, **Gus**, and I.
We sit in the **sun**.
We see **bugs** go by.
That is not **fun**.
Now we sit on a **rug**.
But it is no **fun**.
We sit by the **mud**.
So I get **up**.
Gus does too.
We **jump** and **run**.
This is new.
Look, we like this.
Run, **run**, **run**.
This is good.
Now we can have **fun**.

*/ŭ/ CVC words are identified in bold

Check Progress

Observe student during practice activities and use the following assessment to determine student's success on the target skill. If the student can correctly read two words, consider the intervention successful.

Build a CVC word using the large letter cards. Have a student read it aloud. Continue with the words in the word bank, repeating words when necessary, until each student has successfully read two words.

CVC word bank: bud, cud, dug, fun, mug, nun, tug, rug, rub, mum, bug, sub

Extension Activity

Give each student a copy of the Word Stairs printout and a set of letter tiles (*a, u, r, s, b, h, n, g, t, m*) from the bottom of the Build a Word printout. Give students these instructions and then observe them as they work independently.

1. ***Select three letter tiles to make a real word.***
2. ***Read the word out loud and write the word on the first step.***
3. ***Make a new word with the letter tiles.***
4. ***Read the new word out loud and write the word on the next step.***
5. ***Continue until all the steps are filled.***

If time allows, invite volunteers to talk about two of their words.

Ask: ***How are the words alike? How are they different?***

s	u
m	n

Build a Word

Reteaching Lessons ✓

a	u	r	s	b	h
n	g	t	m		

Name: ______________________________

Gus and I

We want to have fun,
my pup, Gus, and I.
We sit in the sun.
We see bugs go by.

That is not fun.
Now we sit on a rug.
But it is no fun.
We sit by the mud.

So I get up.
Gus does too.
We jump and run.
This is new.

Look, we like this.
Run, run, run.
This is good.
Now we can have fun.

Name: ______________________

Word Stairs

____

____

____

____

____

____

____

____

Reteaching Lessons ✓

Short a: CVCC Pattern

LEARNING OBJECTIVE: Decode regular words formed with short *a*.

LANGUAGE OBJECTIVE: Use phonics clues to sound out words using the short *a* sound.

Lesson Overview

Blend four to six letter words with the short *a* sound. Model vowel-first blending strategy. Play a partner game with spinners to create, write, and decode practice words.

Materials	Preparation
• Letter Cards (*a, l, s, d, h, st, nd, ck, mp*) • Paper clips (one per spinner) • Spinner printout (three spinners per printout)	• Cut out letter cards.

Model

Display Letter Card *a* and ask: ***What letter is this? That's right, this is letter* a.**

Ask: ***Who can tell me the short sound of this vowel?*** Prompt students as needed to say /ă/.

Ask: ***Who can think of a word that has the short sound /ă/?*** If students hesitate, point to available visual cues, such as *hand, map,* or *lamp.*

Explain: ***Let's use what we know about vowel sounds to help us read words carefully. We'll say the sound of the vowel before we read the whole word.***

Use Letter Cards *l, a, and mp* to model vowel-first blending with the word *lamp*. Display *a* and say: ***/ă/.*** Have students repeat the sound.

Explain: ***When we come to this letter in the word, remember to say /ă/.***

Display *l* before *a* and say: ***/l/.*** Have students repeat the sound. Model blending the word through the vowel, sweeping your fingers under the letters as you say the sounds: **/la/.**

Display *mp* after *a* and say: ***/mp/.*** Have students repeat the sound.

Model blending the whole word as you sweep your finger below the letters. Have students blend the sounds and read the word. Have a volunteer use *lamp* in a sentence.

Use Letter Cards to create the words in the word bank, following the process above. Display and say the vowel sound first. Then add cards, blending after each one, to complete the word.

Word bank: *sand, land, lack, dash, hand, last, stamp, past, damp, stack*

Practice and Apply

Have partners work together to create, blend, and read words. Give each student a Spinner printout and a paper clip. Give the following instructions:

One student will hold a pencil tip in the center of the first circle with the paper clip around the point of the pencil.

The other student will spin the clip and then write the letter(s) on the first line of the printout.

Repeat with the next two circles, writing a full word on the first line.

Explain: ***After you have written a word on the line, sound it out the way we practiced.***

Model steps once more as you remind students: ***Say the vowel sound first and then blend from the beginning of the word, remembering the vowel sound when you come to it.***

Have partners decide if the word is real or nonsense. If it is nonsense, have the student cross it out. Have partners take turns and continue until each has a list of four to six real words.

Check Progress

Observe each student during practice and use the following activity to check progress made on the target skill. If student can correctly read two words with short a, consider the intervention successful.

When a pair has completed their lists of words on the Spinner printout, have them trade papers. Listen as each student reads out loud his or her partner's list of words. (If a list does not contain at least two real words with short *a*, the student may need to read from multiple lists.)

Reteaching Lessons

mp

ck

nd

st

h

d

s

l

a

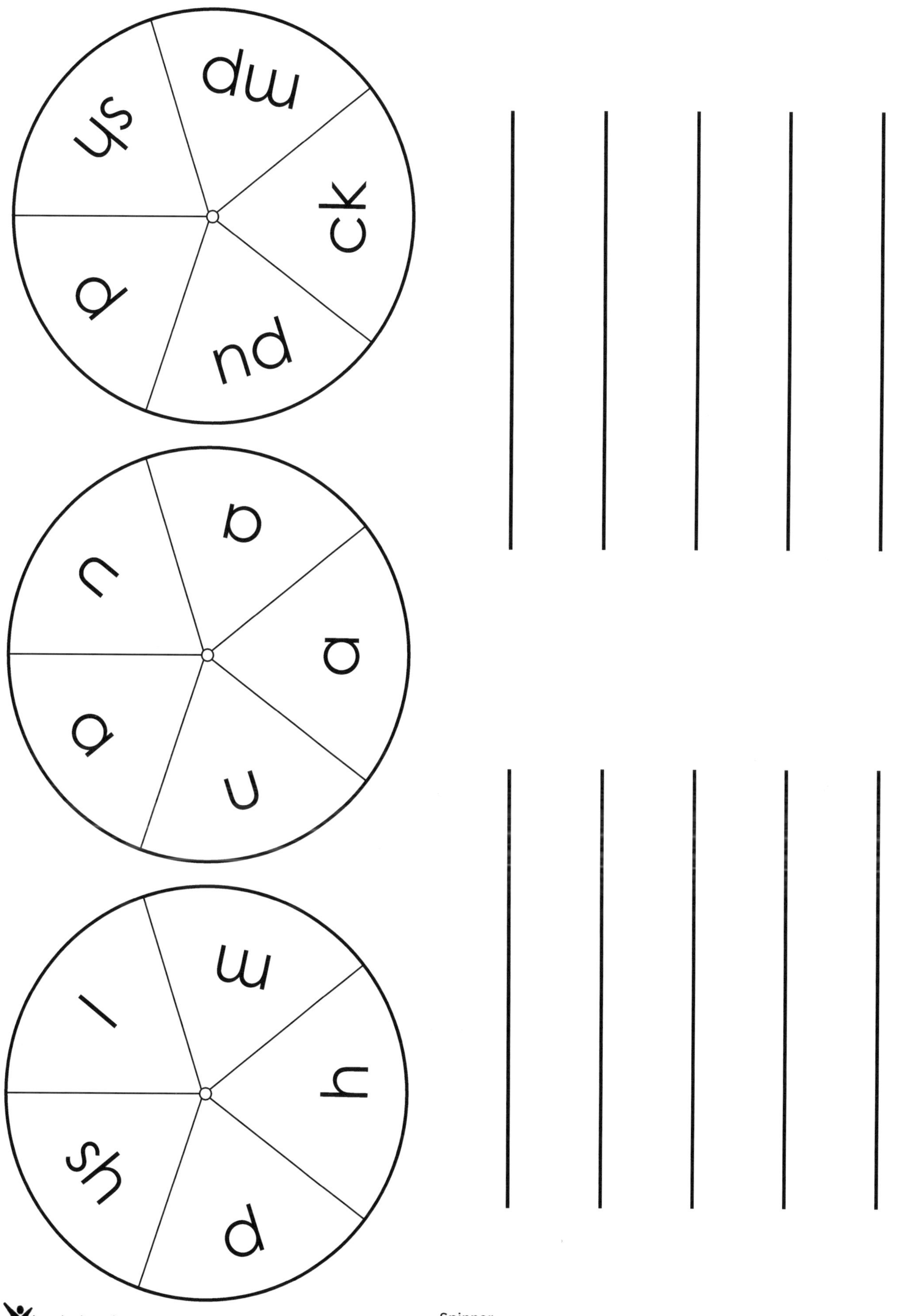

Decodable Words

Short e: CVCC Pattern

LEARNING OBJECTIVE: Decode regular words formed with short e.

LANGUAGE OBJECTIVE: Use phonics clues to sound out words using the short *e* sound.

Lesson Overview

Blend four to six letter words with the short *e* sound. Model vowel-first blending strategy. Play a partner game with spinners to create, write, and decode practice words.

Materials	Preparation
• Letter Cards (*e, n, st, b, p, nd, l, t, nt, ck*) • Paper clips (one per spinner) • Spinner printout (three spinners per printout)	• Cut out letter cards.

Reteaching Lessons

Model

Display Letter Card e and ask: ***What letter is this? That's right, this is letter* e.**

Ask: ***Who can tell me the short sound of this vowel?*** Prompt students as needed to say /ĕ/.

Ask: ***Who can think of a word that has the short sound /ĕ/?*** If students hesitate, point to available visual cues, such as *desk, leg,* or *pen.*

Explain: ***Let's use what we know about vowel sounds to help us read words carefully. We'll say the sound of the vowel before we read the whole word.***

Use Letter Cards *n, e, and st* to model vowel-first blending with the word *nest*. Display *e* and say: **/ĕ/**. Have students repeat the sound.

Explain: ***When we come to this letter in the word, remember to say /ĕ/.***

Display *n* before *e* and say: **/n/**. Have students repeat the sound. Model blending the word through the vowel, sweeping your fingers under the letters as you say the sounds: **/ne/**.

Display *st* after *e* and say: **/st/**. Have students repeat the sound.

Model blending the whole word as you sweep your finger below the letters. Have students blend the sounds and read the word. Have a volunteer use *nest* in a sentence.

Use Letter Cards to create the words in the word bank, following the process above. Display and say the vowel sound first. Then add cards, blending after each one, to complete the word.

Word bank: *best, bend, lend, test, tend, tent, bent, neck, peck, pest*

Practice and Apply

Have partners work together to create, blend, and read words. Give each student a Spinner printout and a paper clip. Give the following instructions:

One student will hold a pencil tip in the center of the first circle with the paper clip around the point of the pencil.

The other student will spin the clip and then write the letter(s) on the first line of the printout.

Repeat with the next two circles, writing a full word on the first line.

Explain: ***After you have written a word on the line, sound it out the way we practiced.***

Model steps once more as you remind students: ***Say the vowel sound first and then blend from the beginning of the word, remembering the vowel sound when you come to it.***

Have partners decide if the word is real or nonsense. If it is nonsense, have the student cross it out. Have partners take turns and continue until each has a list of four to six real words.

Check Progress

Observe each student during practice and use the following activity to check progress made on the target skill. If student can correctly read two words with short e, *consider the intervention successful.*

When a pair has completed their lists of words on the Spinner printout, have them trade papers. Listen as each student reads out loud his or her partner's list of words. (If a list does not contain at least two real words with short e, the student may need to read from multiple lists.)

e	n	b	p	l	t

st	nt	ck	nd

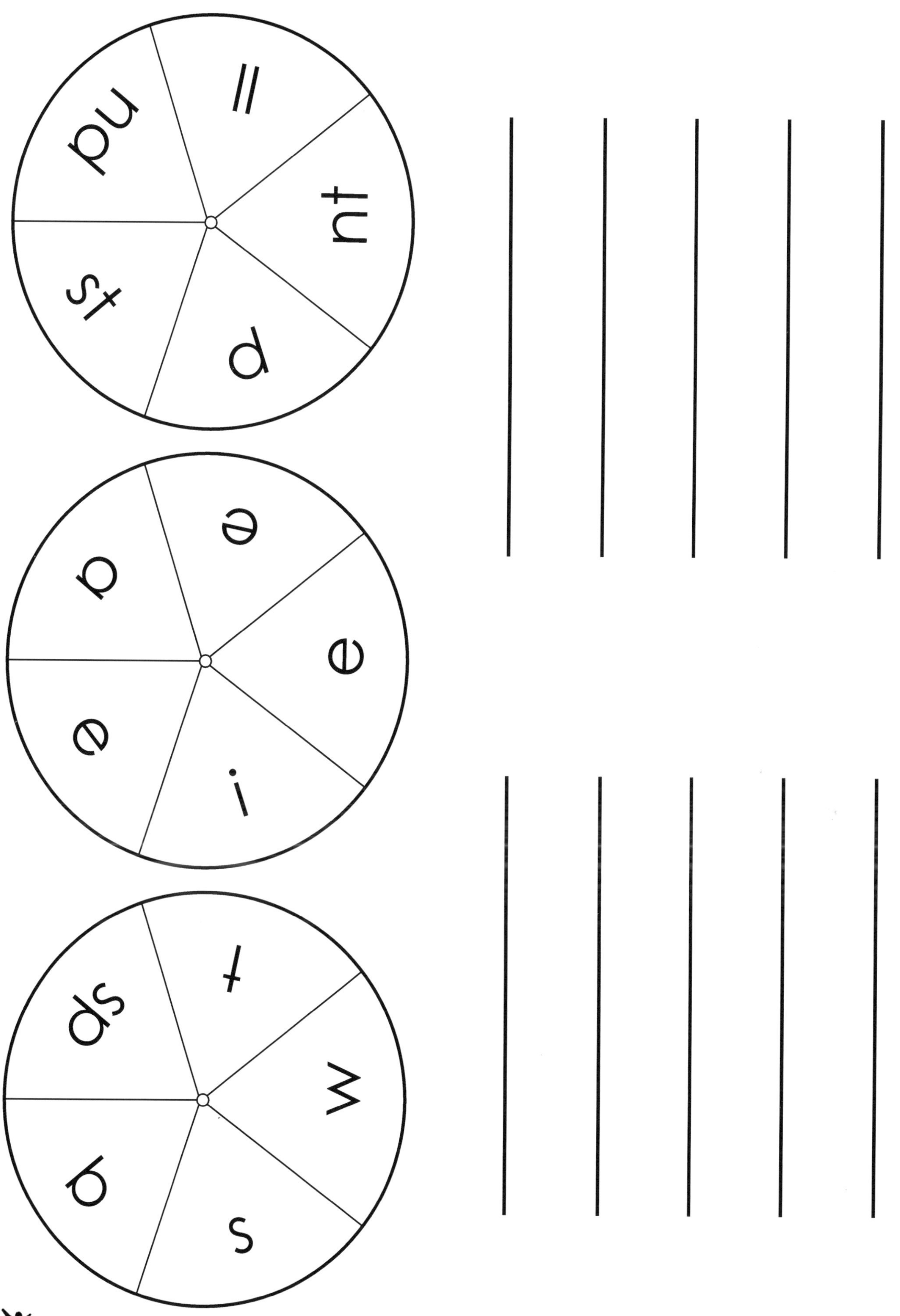

Short i: CVCC Pattern

LEARNING OBJECTIVE: Decode regular words formed with short *i*.

LANGUAGE OBJECTIVE: Use phonics clues to sound out words using the short *i* sound.

Lesson Overview

Blend four to six letter words with the short *i* sound. Model vowel-first blending strategy. Play a partner game with spinners to create, write, and decode practice words.

Materials	Preparation
• Letter Cards (*i, t, p, w, s, m, ck, lk, ll, ss*) • Paper clips (one per spinner) • Spinner printout (three spinners per printout)	• Cut out letter cards.

Model

Display Letter Card *i* and ask: ***What letter is this? That's right, this is letter* i.**

Ask: ***Who can tell me the short sound of this vowel?*** Prompt students as needed to say /ĭ/. ***Who can think of a word that has the short sound /ĭ/?*** If students hesitate, point to available visual cues, such as *lips, pin, or chin..*

Explain: ***Let's use what we know about vowel sounds to help us read words carefully. We'll say the sound of the vowel before we read the whole word.***

Use Letter Cards *s, i, and ck* to model vowel-first blending with the word *sick*. Display *i* and say: **/ĭ/**. Have students repeat the sound.

Explain: ***When we come to this letter in the word, remember to say /ĭ/.***

Display *s* before *i* and say: **/s/**. Have students repeat the sound. Model blending the word through the vowel, sweeping your fingers under the letters as you say the sounds: **/si/**.

Display *ck* after *i* and say: **/ck/**. Have students repeat the sound.

Model blending the whole word as you sweep your finger below the letters. Have students blend the sounds and read the word. Have a volunteer use *sick* in a sentence.

Use Letter Cards to create the words in the word bank, following the process above. Display and say the vowel sound first. Then add cards, blending after each one, to complete the word.

Word bank: *tick, pick, wick, silk, milk, will, sill, pill, miss, kiss*

Practice and Apply

Have partners work together to create, blend, and read words. Give each student a Spinner printout and a paper clip. Give the following instructions:

One student will hold a pencil tip in the center of the first circle with the paper clip around the point of the pencil.

The other student will spin the clip and then write the letter(s) on the first line of the printout.

Repeat with the next two circles, writing a full word on the first line.

Explain: ***After you have written a word on the line, sound it out the way we practiced.***

Model steps once more as you remind students: ***Say the vowel sound first and then blend from the beginning of the word, remembering the vowel sound when you come to it.***

Have partners decide if the word is real or nonsense. If it is nonsense, have the student cross it out. Have partners take turns and continue until each has a list of four to six real words.

Check Progress

Observe each student during practice and use the following activity to check progress made on the target skill. If student can correctly read two words with short i, *consider the intervention successful.*

When a pair has completed their lists of words on the Spinner printout, have them trade papers. Listen as each student reads aloud his or her partner's list of words. (If a list does not contain at least two real words with short *i*, the student may need to read from multiple lists.)

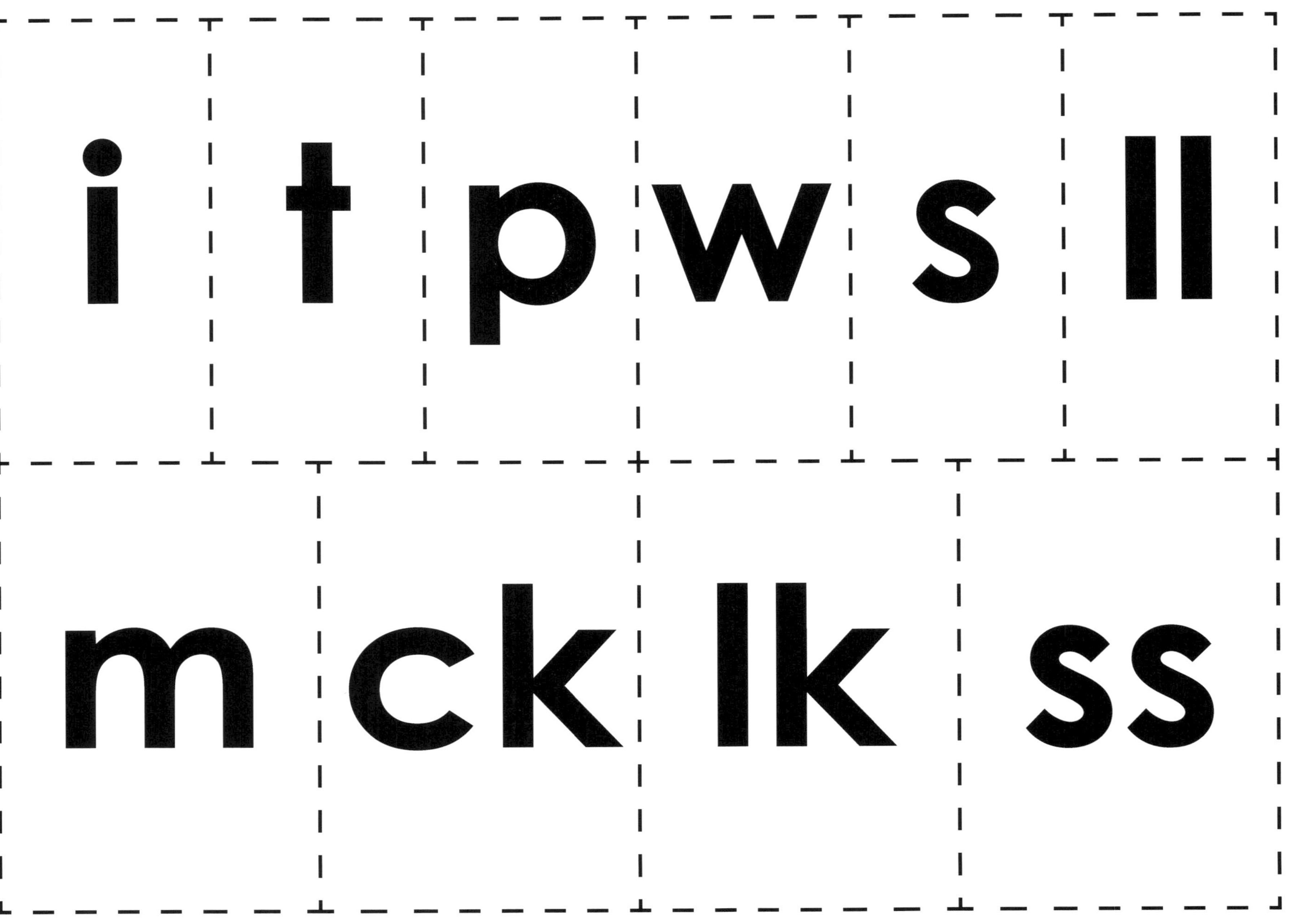
i
t
p
w
s
ll
m
ck
lk
ss

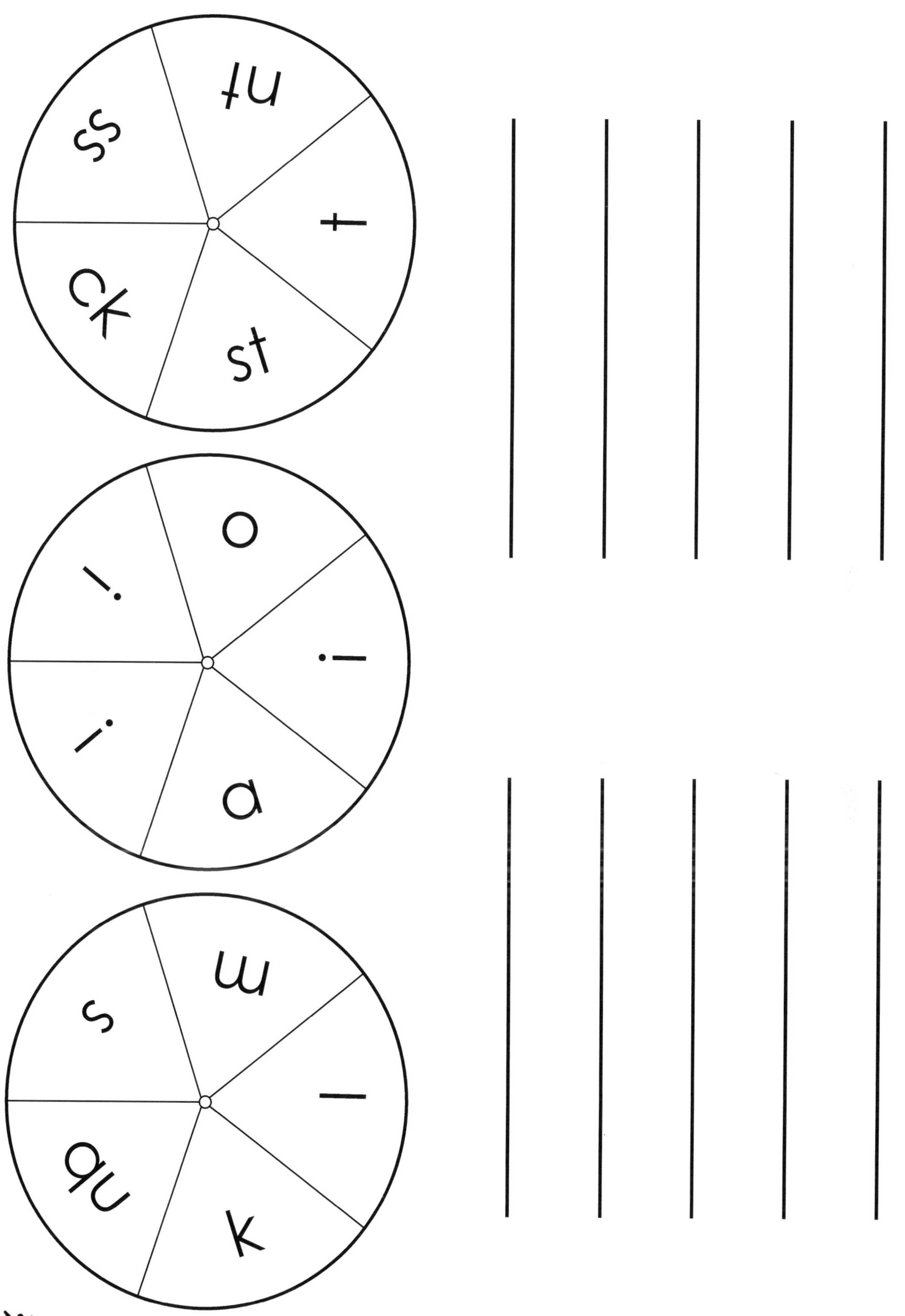

Reteaching Lessons

Decodable Words

Short o: CVCC Pattern

LEARNING OBJECTIVE: Decode regular words formed with short *o*.

LANGUAGE OBJECTIVE: Use phonics clues to sound out words using the short *o* sound.

Lesson Overview

Blend four to six letter words with the short *o* sound. Model vowel-first blending strategy. Play a partner game with spinners to create, write, and decode practice words.

Materials	Preparation
• Letter Cards (*o, l, r, p, st, ck, mp, sh*) • Paper clips (one per spinner) • Spinner printout (three spinners per printout)	• Cut out letter cards.

Model

Display Letter Card *o* and ask: ***What letter is this? That's right, this is letter* o.**

Ask: ***Who can tell me the short sound of this vowel?*** Prompt students as needed to say /ŏ/.

Ask: ***Who can think of a word that has the short sound /ŏ/?*** If students hesitate, point to available visual cues, such as *box, knot, or socks*.

Explain: ***Let's use what we know about vowel sounds to help us read words carefully. We'll say the sound of the vowel before we read the whole word.***

Use Letter Cards *r, o, and ck* to model vowel-first blending with the word *rock*. Display *o* and say: **/ŏ/**. Have students repeat the sound.

Explain: ***When we come to this letter in the word, remember to say /ŏ/.***

Display *r* before *o* and say: **/r/**. Have students repeat the sound. Model blending the word through the vowel, sweeping your fingers under the letters as you say the sounds: **/ro/**.

Display *ck* after *o* and say: **/ck/**. Have students repeat the sound.

Model blending the whole word as you sweep your finger below the letters. Have students blend the sounds and read the word. Have a volunteer use *rock* in a sentence.

Use Letter Cards to create the words in the word bank, following the process above. Display and say the vowel sound first. Then add cards, blending after each one, to complete the word.

Word bank: *lock, lost, romp, stomp, stock, pock, pong, pomp, shock, posh*

Practice and Apply

Have partners work together to create, blend, and read words. Give each student a Spinner printout and a paper clip. Give the following instructions:

One student will hold a pencil tip in the center of the first circle with the paper clip around the point of the pencil.

The other student will spin the clip and then write the letter(s) on the first line of the printout.

Repeat with the next two circles, writing a full word on the first line.

Explain: ***After you have written a word on the line, sound it out the way we practiced.***

Model steps once more as you remind students: ***Say the vowel sound first and then blend from the beginning of the word, remembering the vowel sound when you come to it.***

Have partners decide if the word is real or nonsense. If it is nonsense, have the student cross it out. Have partners take turns and continue until each has a list of four to six real words.

Check Progress

Observe each student during practice and use the following activity to check progress made on the target skill. If student can correctly read two words with short o, *consider the intervention successful.*

When a pair has completed their lists of words on the Spinner printout, have them trade papers. Listen as each student reads aloud his or her partner's list of words. (If a list does not contain at least two real words with short *o*, the student may need to read from multiple lists.)

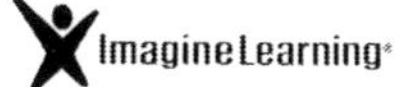

Reteaching Lessons

u

j

l

p

r

f

st

mp

ll

nd

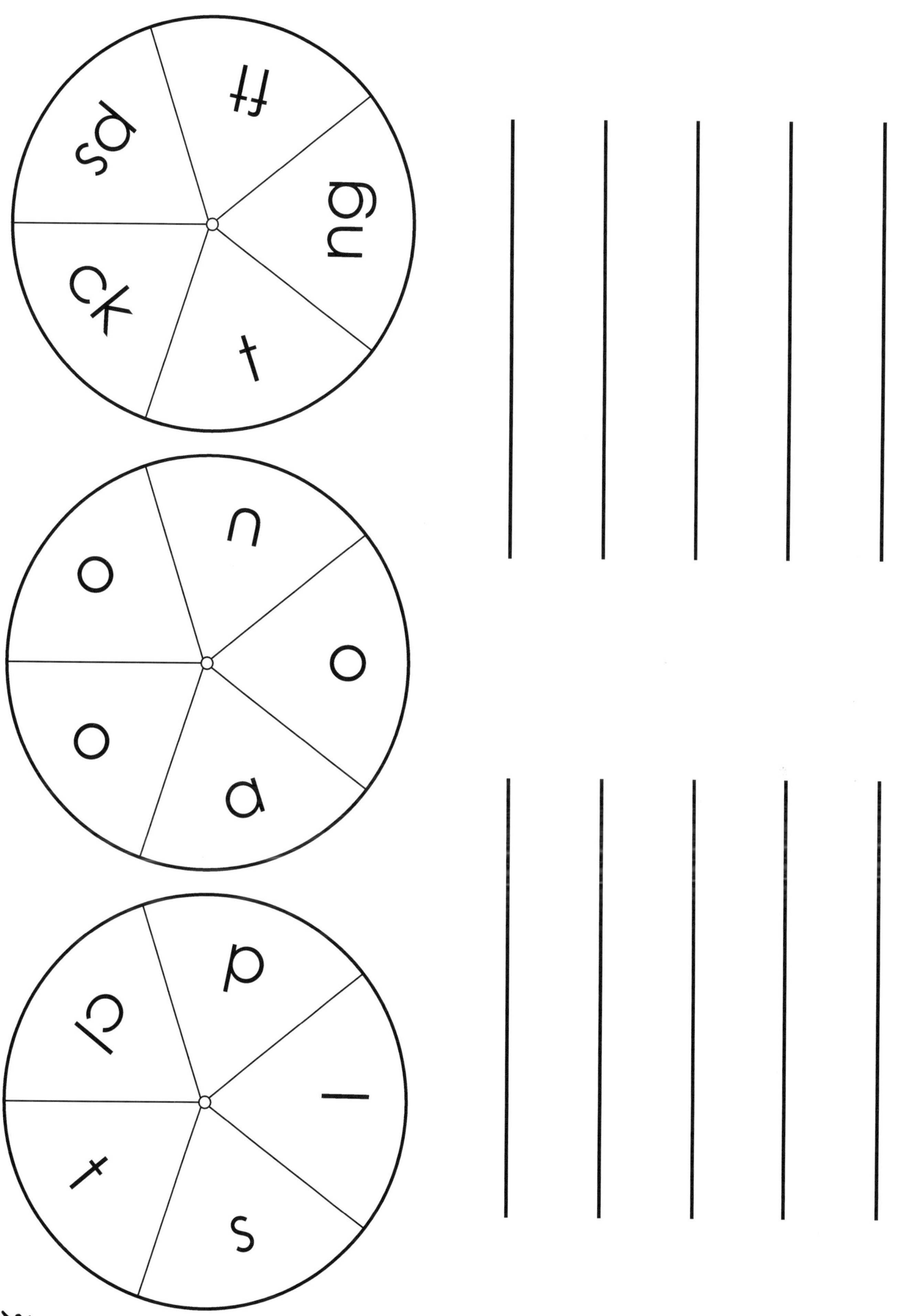
ff
ng
t
ck
ps
u
o
a
o
o
p
l
s
t
cl

Decodable Words

Short u: CVCC Pattern

LEARNING OBJECTIVE: Decode regular words formed with short *u*.
LANGUAGE OBJECTIVE: Use phonics clues to sound out words using the short *u* sound.

Lesson Overview

Blend four to six letter words with the short *u* sound. Model vowel-first blending strategy. Play a partner game with spinners to create, write, and decode practice words.

Materials	Preparation
• Letter Cards (*u, j, l, p, r, f, st, mp, ll, nd*) • Paper clips (one per spinner) • Spinner printout (three spinners per printout)	• Cut out letter cards.

Model

Display Letter Card *u* and ask: ***What letter is this? That's right, this is letter* u.**

Ask: ***Who can tell me the short sound of this vowel?*** Prompt students as needed to say /ŭ/.

Ask: ***Who can think of a word that has the short sound /ŭ/?*** If students hesitate, point to available visual cues, such as *rug, cup, or bun.*

Explain: ***Let's use what we know about vowel sounds to help us read words carefully. We'll say the sound of the vowel before we read the whole word.***

Use Letter Cards *j, u, and mp* to model vowel-first blending with the word *jump*. Display *u* and say: **/ŭ/**. Have students repeat the sound.

Explain: ***When we come to this letter in the word, remember to say /ŭ/.***

Display *j* before *u* and say: **/j/**. Have students repeat the sound. Model blending the word through the vowel, sweeping your fingers under the letters as you say the sounds: **/ju/**.

Display *mp* after *u* and say: **/mp/**. Have students repeat the sound.

Model blending the whole word as you sweep your finger below the letters. Have students blend the sounds and read the word. Have a volunteer use *jump* in a sentence.

Use Letter Cards to create the words in the word bank, following the process above. Display and say the vowel sound first. Then add cards, blending after each one, to complete the word.

Word bank: *pump, lump, stump, rust, just, lull, pull, full, fund*

Practice and Apply

Have partners work together to create, blend, and read words. Give each student a Spinner printout and a paper clip. Give the following instructions:

One student will hold a pencil tip in the center of the first circle with the paper clip around the point of the pencil.

The other student will spin the clip and then write the letter(s) on the first line of the printout.

Repeat with the next two circles, writing a full word on the first line.

Explain: ***After you have written a word on the line, sound it out the way we practiced.***

Model steps once more as you remind students: ***Say the vowel sound first and then blend from the beginning of the word, remembering the vowel sound when you come to it.***

Have partners decide if the word is real or nonsense. If it is nonsense, have the student cross it out. Have partners take turns and continue until each has a list of four to six real words.

Check Progress

Observe each student during practice and use the following activity to check progress made on the target skill. If student can correctly read two words with short u, *consider the intervention successful.*

When a pair has completed their lists of words on the Spinner printout, have them trade papers. Listen as each student reads aloud his or her partner's list of words. (If a list does not contain at least two real words with short *u*, the student may need to read from multiple lists.)

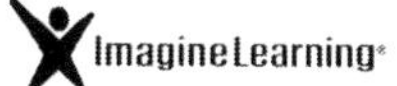

✓ Reteaching Lessons

u	j	l	p	r	f
st		mp	ll		nd

Letter Cards

 Imagine Learning

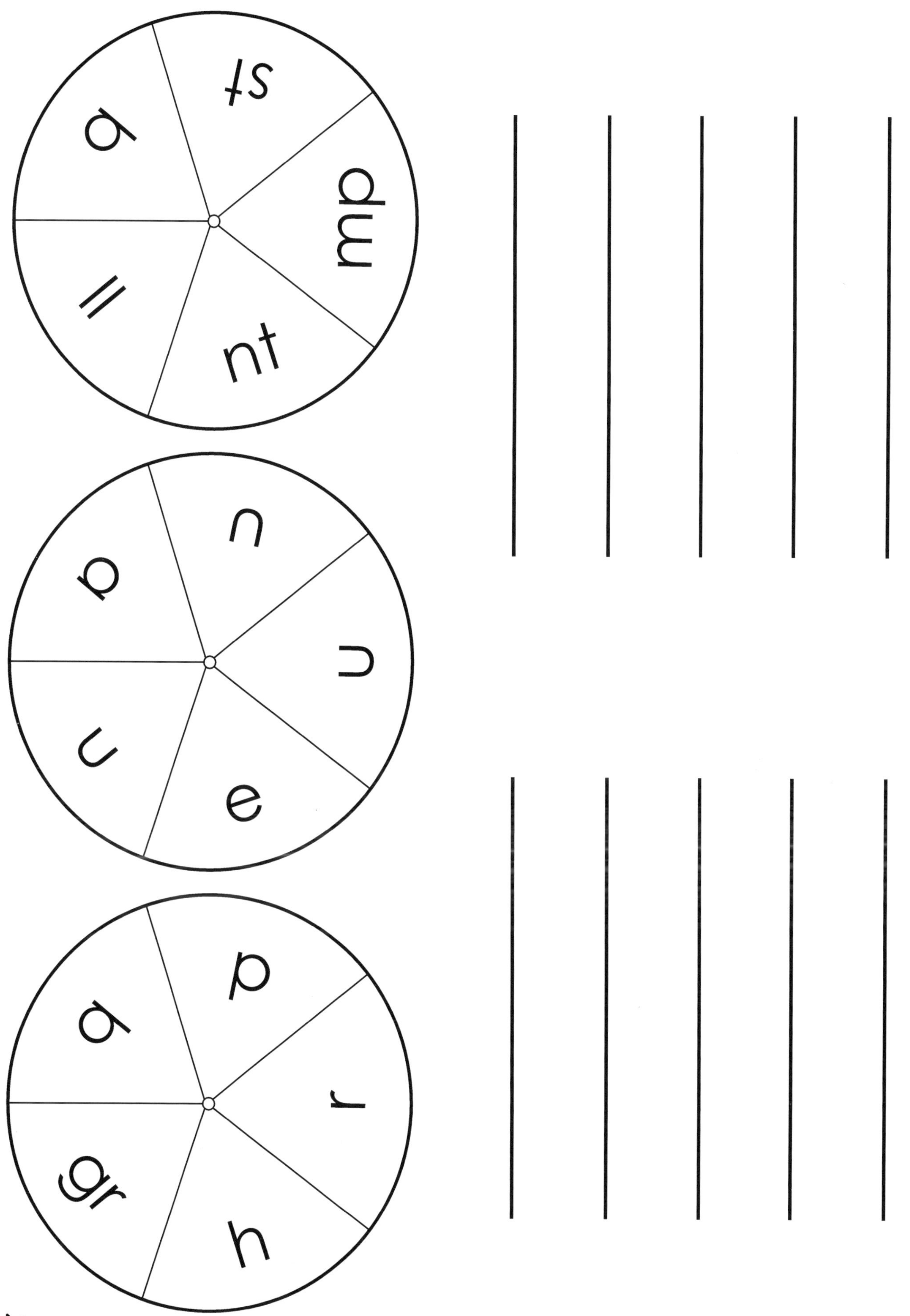
a
st
mp
nt
ll
a
u
n
e
c
a
d
r
h
gr
Reteaching Lessons

Long a: CVCe Pattern

Grade 1

10 min.

CCSS.RF.K.3b
TEKS 110.11.3.B

LEARNING OBJECTIVE: Decode words with the long *a* CVCe (consonant-vowel-consonant-e) pattern.

LANGUAGE OBJECTIVE: Use phonics clues to sound out words that use the long *a* sound and end with silent *e*.

Lesson Overview

Students contrast words with short and long *a* sounds. Using a printout in a wipe-off cover, teacher presents the *_a_e* pattern and students practice common long *a* words that end in silent *e* (consonant-vowel-consonant-e).

Materials	Preparation
• _a_e Word Pattern printout • Clear sheet protector • Dry erase marker and tissues • Sticky notes • Word Cards	• Slide the _a_e Word Pattern printout into a clear sheet protector. • Cut out word cards.

NOTE: To provide a CVC contrast for each CVCe word, one or more practice words may be unknown to students. Focus on the CVCe pattern and the meaning of CVCe target words

Teach and Model

Introduce the long and short vowel sounds for *a*.

Say: ***The letter* a *has a short sound. It is /ă/. It's in words like* fan *and* snack. *Say short* a *with me: /ă/. The letter* a *also has a long sound. It is the same as the vowel's name: /ā/. It's in words like* mane *and* flake. *Say long* a *with me: /ā/.***

Say: ***Now listen to these words:* Man. Mane. *Say them with me:* Man. Mane.**

Ask: ***Which word has the long sound for the letter* a*? Which one has the short sound?*** Prompt students as needed. Repeat process for *Sam* and *same*.

Model comparison activity.

Say: ***I'm going to say a word with the short* a *sound. I want you to think of its long* a *partner word. If I say* mad *you say . . .*** Allow students to say *made*.

Say: ***If I say* lack *you say . . .*** Allow students to say *lake*.

Repeat comparison activity with these words: *snack, snake; back, bake; cap, cape; tap, tape; scrap, scrape; shack, shake*

Say: ***Can you hear how changing from short* a *to long* a *can change the whole word? That's why it is so important to know how to read and write words with long and short* a.**

Introduce the *_a_e* pattern. Display the *_a_e* pattern printout in plastic sheet protector.

Say: ***There are patterns in words that can help you read. Let's look at one pattern. It looks like this.***

Point to the letter *a* and say: ***Here is the letter* a.**

Point to the blanks and say: ***These lines are for consonants.***

Point to the letter *e* and ask: ***What does the* e *at the end tell us?*** Wait for student responses.

Say: ***Right. The* e *at the end is silent but very important. When you see this pattern, you will know that the vowel sound is the same as the vowel's name.***

Model writing a word in the pattern. Write the word *cane* as you say: ***Let's write a word in this pattern. We put a consonant here, /c/, and a consonant here, /n/. We already have the* a *in the middle and the* e *on the end to help make the long vowel sound. What is this word?*** Sweep your finger under the word as you lead students in saying *cane*.

Ask: ***What will happen if there is no* e *at the end?*** Wait for student responses.

Use a sticky note to cover the *e*.

Ask: ***What is this word?*** Prompt students as needed.

Say: ***Yes. Without the*** **e** ***on the end, the vowel in the middle does not say its name and the word is*** **can.** Sweep your finger under the word and lead students in saying *can*.

Erase letters and repeat process for *tape* and *tap*.

Practice and Apply

Say: ***I'll say a long*** **a** ***word, and you tell me the letters we need to fill in the pattern.***

Say: ***The first word is*** **mate.** ***For example, "I can't find the mate to this glove."*** Have students tell you the consonants needed to complete the word.

Ask: ***What is this word?*** Sweep your finger under the word as you lead students in saying *mate*.

Use a sticky note to cover the *e*. Sweep your finger under the word as you lead students in saying *mat*.

Repeat the process with these word pairs: *pane, pan; made, mad; rate, rat; fade, fad; pale, pal; vane, van*

Say: ***There are many words with long a that have more than four letters.*** Draw an extra blank on the pattern card in front of the first blank.

Repeat the above process with these word pairs: *paste, past; state, stat; plane, plan; scrape, scrap*

Check Progress

Observe student during practice activities and use the following assessment to determine student's progress on the target skill. If the student can correctly read two words with the long a pattern, consider the intervention successful.

Show a word card and say: ***When I show you a word, read it out loud. Pay attention to the pattern. Remember, an*** **e** ***at the end of the word tells you that there is a long vowel sound.***

Word Cards: cat, came, fad, face, dad, date, tan, tape, lap, lake, sad, safe

EXTENSION ACTIVITY

Prepare CVCe pattern wipe-off boards for each student by sliding _a_e Word Pattern printouts into sheet protectors. Say words from the word bank and have the students write them into the pattern.

Long a word bank: base, cake, came, date, lane, made, name, save, take, tale, vase, wake, wave, flame, flake, shape, stake, chase, shave, skate

Reteaching Lessons

Reteaching Lessons

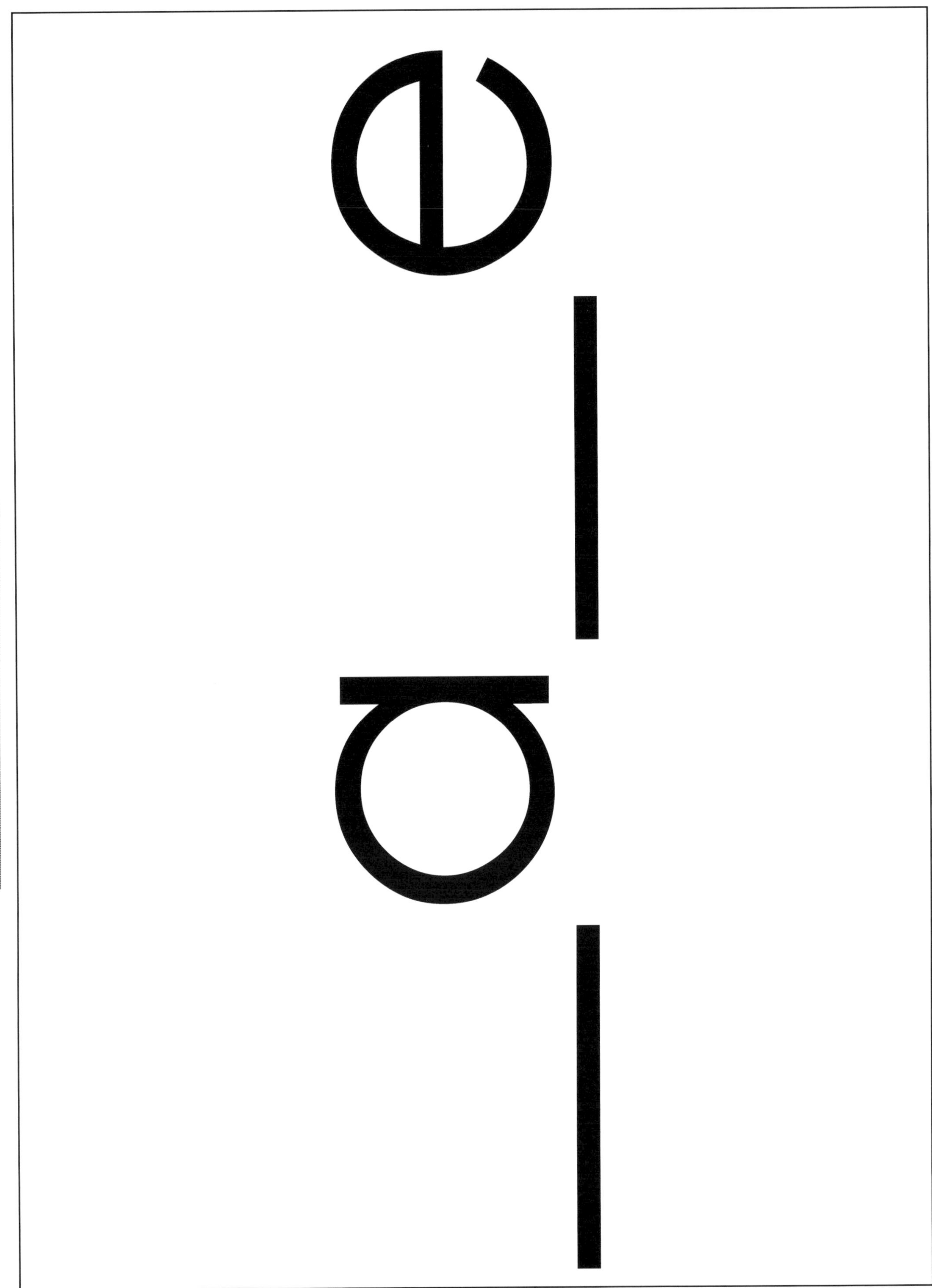

cat	came
fad	face
dad	date
tan	tape
lap	lake
sad	safe

Decodable Words

Long i: CVCe Pattern

Grade 1

10 min.

CCSS.RF.K.3b
TEKS 110.11.3.B

LEARNING OBJECTIVE: Decode words with the long *i* CVCe (consonant-vowel-consonant-e) pattern.

LANGUAGE OBJECTIVE: Use phonics clues to sound out words that use the long *i* sound and end with silent *e*.

Lesson Overview

Students contrast words with short and long *i* sounds. Using a printout in a wipe-off cover, teacher presents the _*i*_*e* pattern and students practice common long *i* words that end in silent *e* (consonant-vowel-consonant-e).

Materials	Preparation
• _i_e Word Pattern printout • Clear sheet protector • Dry erase marker and tissues • Sticky notes • Word Cards	• Slide the _i_e Word Pattern printout into a clear sheet protector. • Cut out word cards.

 NOTE: To provide a CVC contrast for each CVCe word, the practice activity may contain one or more practice words that are unfamiliar to students. Focus on the CVCe pattern and the meaning of CVCe target words.

Reteaching Lessons

Teach and Model

Introduce the long and short vowel sounds for *i*.

Say: ***The letter* i *has a short sound. It is /ĭ/. It's in words like* big *and* stick. *Say short* i *with me: /ĭ/. The letter* i *also has a long sound. It is the same as the vowel's name: /ī/. It's in words like* ice *and* five. *Say long* i *with me: /ī/.***

Say: ***Now listen to these words:* Dim. Dime. *Say them with me:* Dim. Dime.**

Ask: ***Which word has the long sound for the letter* i*? Which one has the short sound?*** Prompt students as needed. Repeat process for *spit* and *spite*.

Model comparison activity.

Say: ***I'm going to say a word with the short* i *sound. I want you to think of its long* i *partner word. If I say* fill, *you say . . .*** Allow students to say *file*.

Say: ***If I say* bit, *you say . . .*** Allow students to say *bite*.

Repeat comparison activity with these words: *miss, mice; slid, slide; sit, site; Tim, time; trick, trike*

Say: ***Can you hear how changing from short* i *to long* i *can change the whole word? That's why it is so important to know how to read and write words with long and short* i.**

Introduce the _*i*_*e* pattern. Display the _*i*_*e* pattern printout in plastic sheet protector.

Say: ***There are patterns in words that can help you read. Let's look at one pattern. It looks like this.***

Point to the letter *i* and say: ***Here is the letter* i.**

Point to the blanks and say: ***These lines are for consonants.***

Point to the letter *e* and ask: ***What does the* e *at the end tell us?*** Wait for student responses.

Say: ***Right. The* e *at the end is silent but very important. When you see this pattern, you will know that the vowel sound is the same as the vowel's name.***

Model writing a word in the pattern. Write the word *kite* as you say: ***Let's write a word in this pattern. We put a consonant here, /k/, and a consonant here, /t/. We already have the* i *in the middle and the* e *on the end to help make the long vowel sound. What is this word?*** Sweep your finger under the word as you lead students in saying *kite*.

Ask: ***What will happen if there is no* e *at the end?*** Wait for student responses.

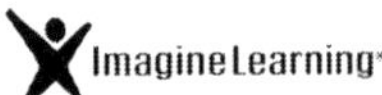

Use a sticky note to cover the *e*.

Ask: ***What is this word?*** Prompt students as needed.

Say: ***Yes. Without the* e *on the end, the vowel in the middle does not say its name and the word is* kit.** Sweep your finger under the word and lead students in saying *kit*.

Erase letters and repeat process for *dine* and *din*.

Practice and Apply

Say: ***I'll say a long* i *word, and you tell me the letters we need to fill in the pattern.***

Say: ***The first word is* ride. *For example, "I wear a helmet when I ride my bike."*** Have students tell you the consonants needed to complete the word.

Ask: ***What is this word?*** Sweep your finger under the word as you lead students in saying *ride*.

Use a sticky note to cover the *e*. Sweep your finger under the word as you lead students in saying *rid*.

Repeat the process with these word pairs: *ripe, rip; pine, pin; hide, hid; bide, bid; fine, fin; bite, bit*

Say: ***There are many words with long i that have more than four letters.*** Draw an extra blank on the pattern card in front of the first blank.

Repeat the above process with these word pairs: *shine, shin; twine, twin; spine, spin; quite, quit*

Check Progress

Observe student during practice activities and use the following assessment to determine student's progress on the target skill. If the student can correctly read two words with the long i *pattern, consider the intervention successful.*

Show a word card and say: ***When I show you a word, read it out loud. Pay attention to the pattern. Remember, an* e *at the end of the word tells you that there is a long vowel sound.***

Word Cards: bib, bike, tile, tip, lid, line, fit, fine, sit, size, did, dive

EXTENSION ACTIVITY

Prepare CVCe pattern wipe-off boards for each student by sliding _i_e Word Pattern printouts into sheet protectors. Say words from the word bank and have the students write them into the pattern.

Long i *word bank*: five, bike, life, lime, mile, smile, wide, rice, like, mine, pride, slime, glide, wipe, stripe, hive, pile

Reteaching Lessons

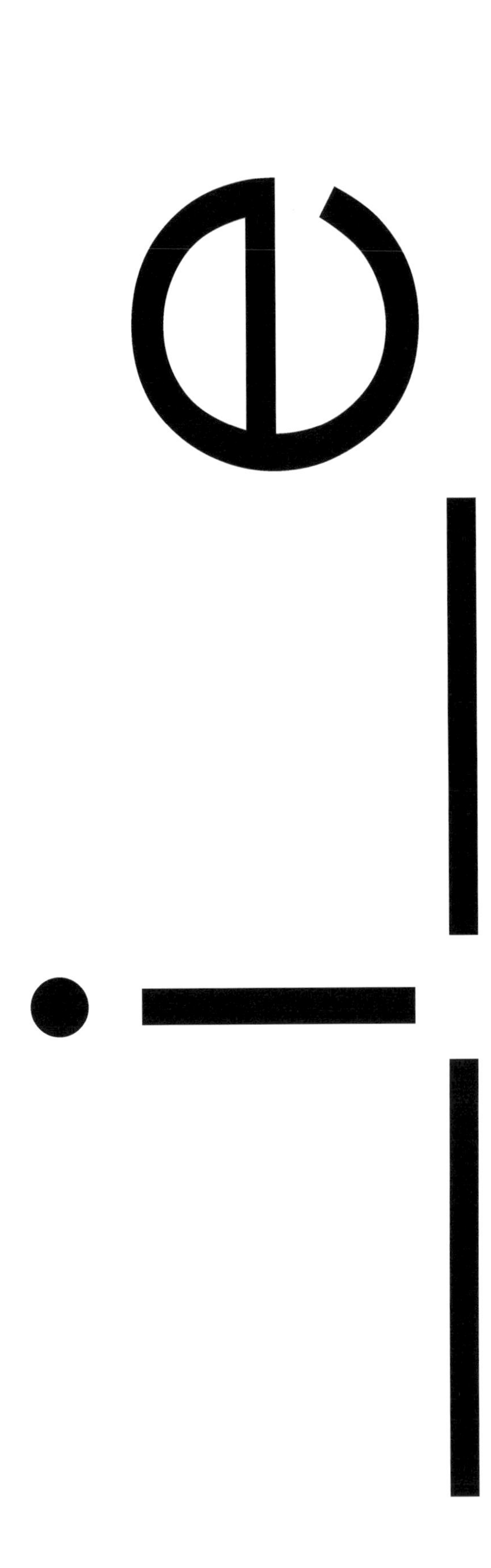

ImagineLearning

bib	bike
tile	tip
lid	line
fit	fine
sit	size
did	dive

Reteaching Lessons ✓

Decodable Words

Long o: CVCe Pattern

Grade 1
10 min.

CCSS.RF.K.3b
TEKS 110.11.3.B

LEARNING OBJECTIVE: Decode words with the long *o* CVCe (consonant-vowel-consonant-e) pattern.

LANGUAGE OBJECTIVE: Use phonics clues to sound out words that use the long *o* sound and end with silent *e*.

Lesson Overview

Students contrast words with short and long *o* sounds. Using a printout in a wipe-off cover, teacher presents the _*o*_*e* pattern and students practice common long *o* words that end in silent *e* (consonant-vowel-consonant-e).

Materials	Preparation
• _o_e Word Pattern printout • Clear sheet protector • Dry erase marker and tissues • Sticky notes • Word Cards	• Slide the _o_e Word Pattern printout into a clear sheet protector. • Cut out word cards.

NOTE: To provide a CVC contrast for each CVCe word, the practice activity may contain one or more practice words that are unfamiliar to students. Focus on the CVCe pattern and the meaning of CVCe target words.

Teach and Model

Introduce the long and short vowel sounds for *o*.

Say: ***The letter* o *has a short sound. It is /ŏ/. It's in words like* dog *and* sock. *Say short* o *with me: /ŏ/. The letter* o *also has a long sound. It is the same as the vowel's name: /ō/. It's in words like* phone *and* note. *Say long* o *with me: /ō/.***

Say: ***Now listen to these words:* Hop. Hope. *Say them with me:* Hop. Hope.**

Ask: ***Which word has the long sound for the letter* o*? Which one has the short sound?*** Prompt students as needed. Repeat process for *pop* and *pope*.

Model comparison activity.

Say: ***I'm going to say a word with the short* o *sound. I want you to think of its long* o *partner word. If I say* cod, *you say . . .*** Allow students to say *code*.

Say: ***If I say* rod, *you say . . .*** Allow students to say *rode*.

Repeat comparison activity with these words: *dot, dote; lop, lope; wok, woke; glob, globe*

Say: ***Can you hear how changing from short* o *to long* o *can change the whole word? That's why it is so important to know how to read and write words with long and short* o.**

Introduce the _*o*_*e* pattern. Display the _*o*_*e* pattern printout in plastic sheet protector.

Say: ***There are patterns in words that can help you read. Let's look at one pattern. It looks like this.***

Point to the letter *o* and say: ***Here is the letter* o.**

Point to the blanks and say: ***These lines are for consonants.***

Point to the letter *e* and ask: ***What does the* e *at the end tell us?*** Wait for student responses.

Say: ***Right. The* e *at the end is silent but very important. When you see this pattern, you will know that the vowel sound is the same as the vowel's name.***

Model writing a word in the pattern. Write the word *robe* as you say: ***Let's write a word in this pattern. We put a consonant here, /r/, and a consonant here, /b/. We already have the* o *in the middle and the* e *on the end to help make the long vowel sound. What is this word?*** Sweep your finger under the word as you lead students in saying *robe*.

Ask: ***What will happen if there is no* e *at the end?*** Wait for student responses.

Use a sticky note to cover the *e*.

Ask: ***What is this word?*** Prompt students as needed.

Say: ***Yes. Without the* e *on the end, the vowel in the middle does not say its name and the word is* rob.** Sweep your finger under the word and lead students in saying *mod*.

Erase letters and repeat process for *cop* and *cope*.

Practice and Apply

Say: ***I'll say a long* o *word, and you tell me the letters we need to fill in the pattern.***

Say: ***The first word is* lobe. *For example, "My ears have big lobes."*** Have students tell you the consonants needed to complete the word.

Ask: ***What is this word?*** Sweep your finger under the word as you lead students in saying *lobe*.

Use a sticky note to cover the *e*. Sweep your finger under the word as you lead students in saying *lob*.

Repeat the process with these word pairs: *cone, con; mode, mod; mope, mop; hope, hop; note, not*

Say: ***There are many words with long* o *that have more than four letters.*** Draw an extra blank on the pattern card in front of the first blank.

Repeat the above process with these word pairs: *slope, slop; globe, glob*

Check Progress

Observe student during practice activities and use the following assessment to determine student's progress on the target skill. If the student can correctly read two words with the long o pattern, consider the intervention successful.

Show a word card and say: ***When I show you a word, read it out loud. Pay attention to the pattern. Remember, an* e *at the end of the word tells you that there is a long vowel sound.***

Word Cards: joke, job, nose, not, rope, rock, home, hot, lone, log, cove, cod

EXTENSION ACTIVITY

Prepare CVCe pattern wipe-off boards for each student by sliding the _*o*_*e* Word Pattern printout into sheet protectors. Say words from the word bank and have the students write them into the pattern.

Long o word bank: role, pole, zone, lone, vote, yoke, rose, dome, nope, bone, broke, choke, close, smoke

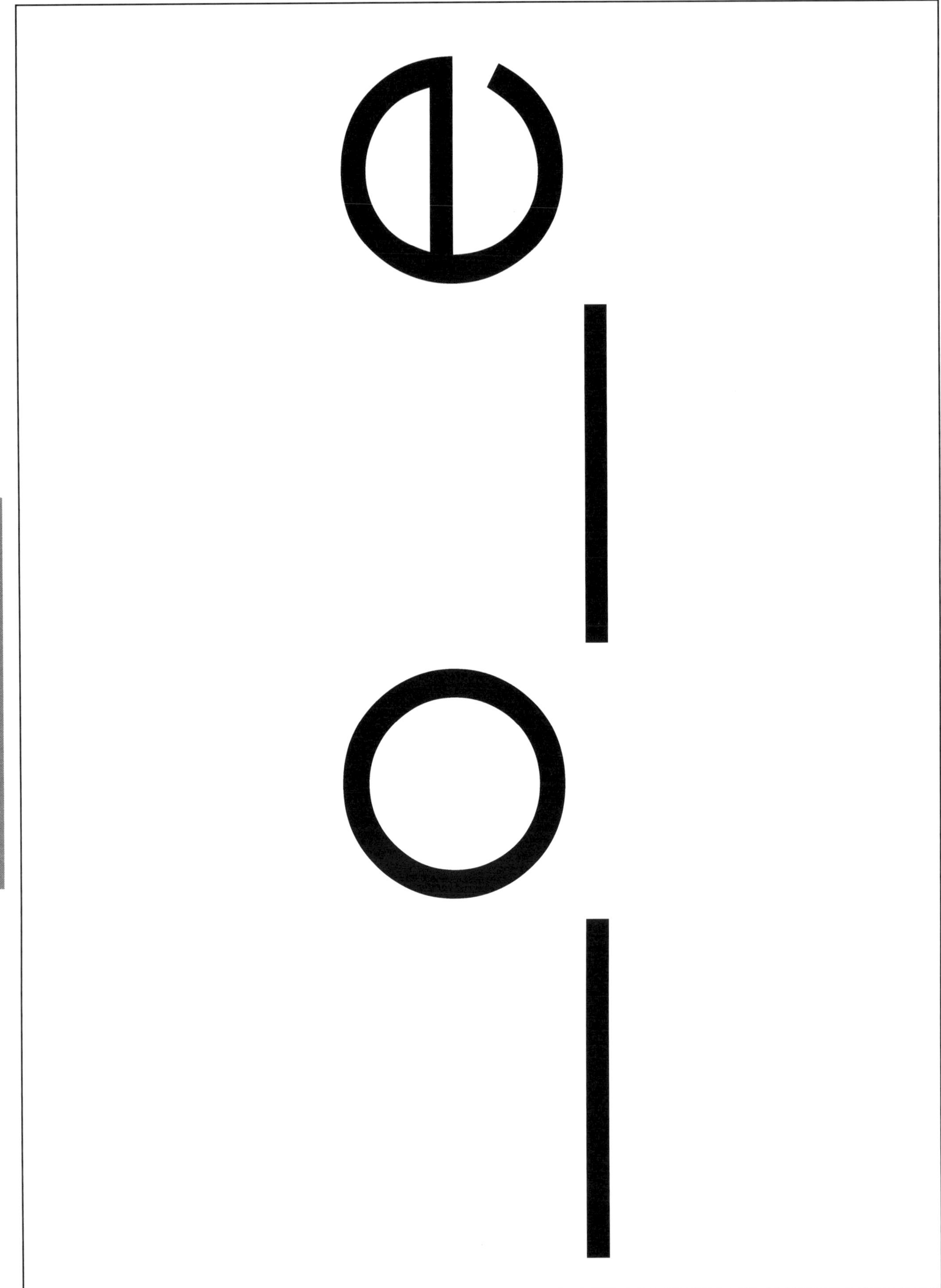
_o_e

job	joke
not	nose
rock	rope
hot	home
log	lone
cod	cove

Reteaching Lessons ✓

Long u: CVCe Pattern

Grade 1

10 min.

CCSS.RF.K.3b
TEKS 110.11.3.B

LEARNING OBJECTIVE: Decode words with the long *u* CVCe (consonant-vowel-consonant-e) pattern.

LANGUAGE OBJECTIVE: Use phonics clues to sound out words that use the long *u* sound and end with silent *e*.

Lesson Overview

Students contrast words with short and long *u* sounds. Using a printout in a wipe-off cover, teacher presents the _*u*_*e* pattern and students practice common long *u* words that end in silent *e* (consonant-vowel-consonant-e).

Materials	Preparation
• _u_e Word Pattern printout • Clear sheet protector • Dry erase marker and tissues • Sticky notes • Word Cards	• Slide the _u_e Word Pattern printout into a clear sheet protector. • Cut out Word Cards.

NOTE: To provide a CVC contrast for each CVCe word, the practice activity may contain one or more practice words that are unfamiliar to students. Focus on the CVCe pattern and the meaning of CVCe target words.

Teach and Model

Introduce the long and short vowel sounds for *u*.

Say: ***The letter* u *has a short sound. It is /ŭ/. It's in words like* bus *and* truck. *Say short* u *with me: /ŭ/. The letter* u *also has a long sound. It is the same as the vowel's name: /ū/. It's in words like* flute *and* tune. *Say long* u *with me: /ū/.***

Say: ***Now listen to these words:* Duck. Duke. *Say them with me:* Duck. Duke.**

Ask: ***Which word has the long sound for the letter* u*? Which one has the short sound?*** Prompt students as needed. Repeat process for *mutt* and *mute*.

Say: ***Can you hear how changing from short* u *to long* u *can change the whole word? That's why it is so important to know how to read and write words with long and short* u.**

Introduce the _*u*_*e* pattern. Display the _*u*_*e* pattern printout in plastic sheet protector.

Say: ***There are patterns in words that can help you read. Let's look at one pattern. It looks like this.***

Point to the letter *u* and say: ***Here is the letter* u.**

Point to the blanks and say: ***These lines are for consonants.***

Point to the letter *e* and ask: ***What does the* e *at the end tell us?*** Wait for student responses.

Say: ***Right. The* e *at the end is silent but very important. When you see this pattern, you will know that the vowel sound is the same as the vowel's name.***

Model writing a word in the pattern. Write the word *cube* as you say: ***Let's write a word in this pattern. We put a consonant here, /c/, and a consonant here, /b/. We already have the* u *in the middle and the* e *on the end to help make the long vowel sound. What is this word?*** Sweep your finger under the word as you lead students in saying *cube*.

Ask: ***What will happen if there is no* e *at the end?*** Wait for student responses.

Use a sticky note to cover the *e*.

Ask: ***What is this word?*** Prompt students as needed.

Say: ***Yes. Without the* e *on the end, the vowel in the middle does not say its name and the word is* cub.** Sweep your finger under the word and lead students in saying *cub.*

Erase letters and repeat process for *rune* and *run.*

Practice and Apply

Say: ***I'll say a long* u *word, and you tell me the letters we need to fill in the pattern.***

Say: ***The first word is* tube. *For example, "Toothpaste comes in a tube."*** Have students tell you the consonants needed to complete the word.

Ask: ***What is this word?*** Sweep your finger under the word as you lead students in saying *tube.*

Use a sticky note to cover the *e.* Sweep your finger under the word as you lead students in saying *tub.*

Repeat the process with these word pairs: *cute, cut; huge, hug; rude, rud; mule; mul; tune, tun*

Check Progress

Observe student during practice activities and use the following assessment to determine student's progress on the target skill. If the student can correctly read two words with the long u *pattern, consider the intervention successful.*

Show a word card and say: ***When I show you a word, read it out loud. Pay attention to the pattern. Remember, an* e *at the end of the word tells you that there is a long vowel sound.***

Word Cards: duke, dud, tune, tub, mute, mud, cube, cups, plume, plug, dupe, duck

EXTENSION ACTIVITY

Prepare CVCe pattern wipe-off boards for each student by sliding the *_u_e* Word Pattern printout into sheet protectors. Say words from the word bank and have the students write them into the pattern.

Long u *word bank*: rude, lute, dune, duke, flute, fume, rule, brute, muse, prune, fuse, truce

Reteaching Lessons

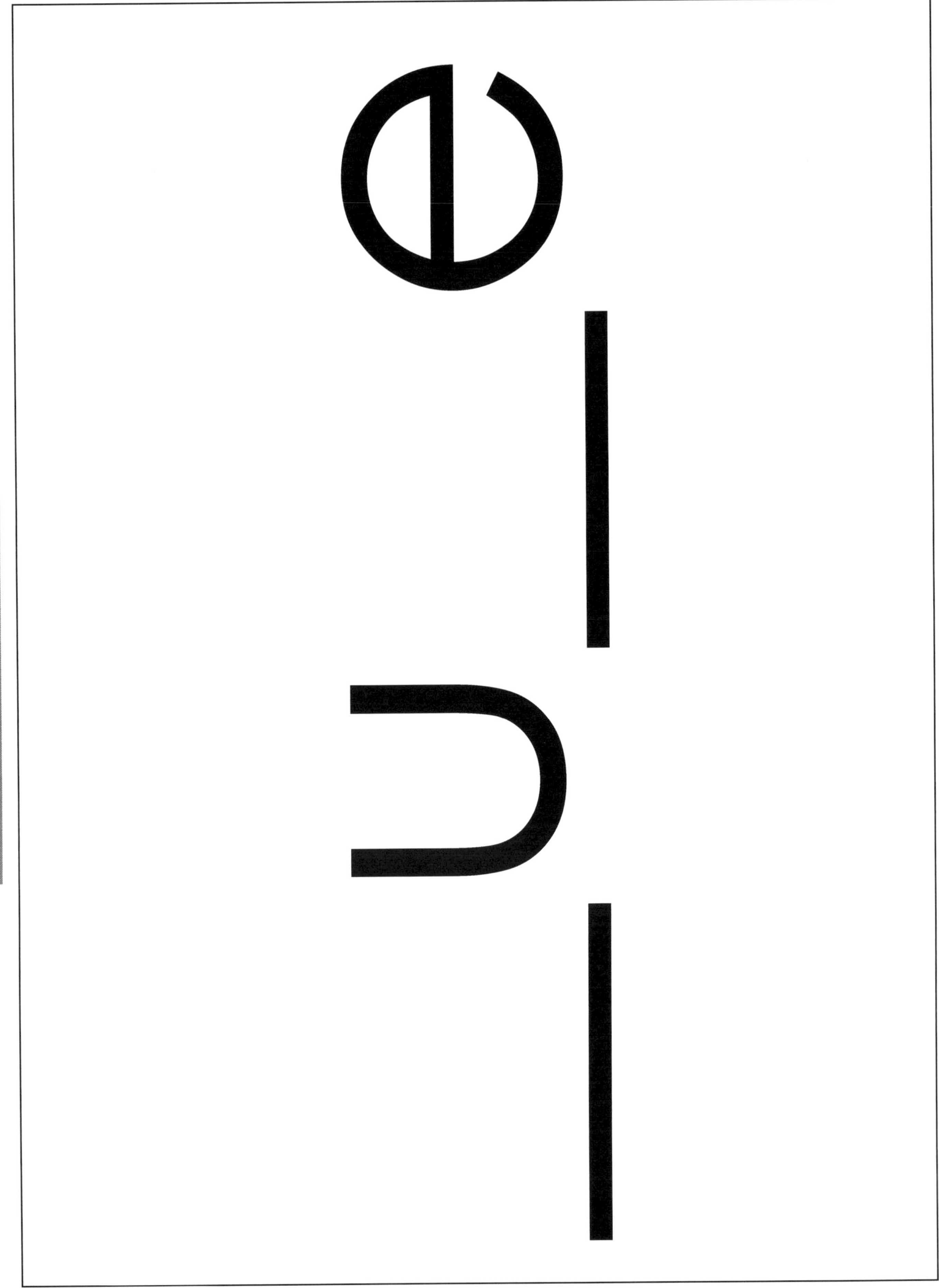
_u_e

dud	duke
tub	tune
mud	mute
cups	cube
plug	plume
duck	dupe

Reteaching Lessons ✓

Decodable Words

Words with ay and ai

Grade 1

15 min.

CCSS.RF.K.3b
TEKS 110.11.3.B

LEARNING OBJECTIVE: Decode words using the long *a* sound formed with the vowel teams *ay* and *ai*.

LANGUAGE OBJECTIVE: Use phonics clues to sound out words using the long *a* sound formed with the vowel teams *ay* and *ai*.

Lesson Overview

Teacher reviews the *ay* and *ai* vowel teams. Students use letter tiles to add consonants to the vowel teams and to create words. As a review, students read out loud the list of words created.

Materials	Preparation
• Letter Tiles • Small box or a bag	• Cut out Letter Tiles. • Place consonant tiles in a small box or bag. (Reserve vowel team tiles for instruction.)

Teach Long a Vowel Teams

Ask: ***Who can tell me the sound for long* a*? (/ā/)*** Have students repeat /ā/.

Remind students: ***In a vowel team, two letters work together to stand for the long vowel sound.***

Ask: ***Who can name one of the vowel teams for the long a sound? Who can name the other vowel team?***

Display the *ay* tile and elaborate: **Ay *is a long* a *vowel team. The letters* a *and* y *work together to make the long sound /ā/.*** Have students repeat the long *A* sound.

Display the *ai* tile and elaborate: **Ai *is a long* a *vowel team. The letters* a *and* i *work together to make the long sound /ā/.*** Have students repeat the long *a* sound.

Practice and Apply

Demonstrate: Place the *ay* tile on the table and say: ***Let's add letters to the long* a *teams to make words. In this bag I have some letter tiles. These letters are consonants. I will draw a letter from the bag and add it to* ay *to see if I can make a word.***

Have students draw tiles and create three-letter words. Guide them as needed. For example: ***Is that a word? Let's sound it out.*** Sweep your finger under the word. **/d/ /ā/ ... day.** ***Is it a word?*** Write the word on the whiteboard and have students repeat it with you.

Continue the activity. Have students draw new tiles and create new three-letter words. As words are completed, write them on the whiteboard and have students repeat them with you. After a few turns, challenge students to try adding a new tile to the last word created to see if they can make a four-letter word.

After students have created five or six words, change from *ay* to *ai*. Place the *ai* tile on the table and explain: ***For the* ai *team words, you can draw two tiles at a time. Try using one letter before the team and one after to make a four-letter word.***

After a few turns, challenge students to try adding a new tile to the last word created to see if they can make a five-letter word. Write all words on the whiteboard and have students repeat them with you.

Check Progress

Observe each student during practice and use the following activity to check progress made on the target skill. If student can read a word from each team, consider the intervention successful.

Display the list of words you have created. Explain: ***I will name a vowel team. Look at the list to find and read aloud one word with that vowel team.*** Demonstrate the task using a sample word from the list on the board. Alternate between vowel teams, giving each student several opportunities to read words.

ai	ay	d	n
p	l	s	r
t	w	m	b
h	c	j	f

Reteaching Lessons ✓

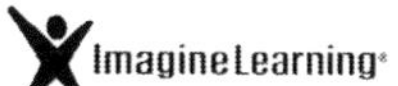

Decodable Words

Words with ea and ee

Grade 1

15 min.

CCSS.RF.K.3b
TEKS 110.11.3.B

LEARNING OBJECTIVE: Decode words using the long *e* sound formed with the vowel teams *ea* and *ee*.

LANGUAGE OBJECTIVE: Use phonics clues to sound out words using the long *e* sound formed with the vowel teams *ea* and *ee*.

Lesson Overview

Teacher reviews the *ea* and *ee* vowel teams. Students use letter tiles to add consonants to the vowel teams and to create words. As a review, students read aloud the list of words created.

Materials	Preparation
• Letter Tiles • Small box or a bag	• Cut out Letter Tiles. • Place consonant tiles in a small box or bag. (Reserve vowel team tiles for instruction.)

Teach Long e Vowel Teams

Ask: ***Who can tell me the sound for long* e? (/ē/)** Have students repeat /ē/.

Remind students: ***In a vowel team, two letters work together to stand for the long vowel sound.***

Ask: ***Who can name one of the vowel teams for the long e sound? Who can name the other vowel team?***

Display the *ea* tile and elaborate: **Ea *is a long* e *vowel team. The letters* e *and* a *work together to make the long sound /ē/.*** Have students repeat the long *e* sound.

Display the *ee* tile and elaborate: **Ee *is a long* e *vowel team. The letters* e *and* e *work together to make the long sound /ē/.*** Have students repeat the long *e* sound.

Practice and Apply

Demonstrate: Place the *ee* tile on the table and say: ***Let's add letters to the long e teams to make words. In this bag I have some letter tiles. These letters are consonants. I will draw two letters from the bag and add them to* ee *to see if I can make a word. I can add them before or after the vowel team.***

Have students draw tiles and create words. Guide them as needed. For example: ***Is that a word? Let's sound it out.*** Sweep your finger under the word. **/b/ /ē/ /p/ ... beep. *Is it a word?*** Write the word on the whiteboard and have students repeat it with you.

Continue the activity. Have students draw new tiles and create new words. Replace tiles in bag as needed. As words are completed, write them on the whiteboard and have students repeat them with you. After a few turns, challenge students to try adding a new tile to the last word created to see if they can make a five-letter word.

After students have created five or six words, change from *ee* to *ea*. Place the *ea* tile on the table. Have students draw new tiles and create new words. Replace tiles in bag as needed. As words are completed, write them on the whiteboard and have students repeat them with you.

After a few turns, challenge students to try adding a new tile to the last word created to see if they can make a five letter word. Write all words on the whiteboard and have students repeat them with you.

Check Progress

Observe each student during practice and use the following activity to check progress made on the target skill. If student can read a word from each team, consider the intervention successful.

Display the list of words you have created. Explain: ***I will name a vowel team. Look at the list to find and read out loud one word with that vowel team.*** Demonstrate the task using a sample word from the list on the board. Alternate between vowel teams, giving each student several opportunities to read words.

ea	ee	t	r
m	n	l	s
d	f	b	p
h	w	k	c

Reteaching Lessons

Decodable Words

Words with igh

Grade 1

15 min.

CCSS.RF.K.3b
TEKS 110.11.3.B

LEARNING OBJECTIVE: Decode words using the long *i* sound formed with the vowel team *igh*.

LANGUAGE OBJECTIVE: Use phonics clues to sound out words using the long *i* sound formed with the vowel team *igh*.

Lesson Overview

Teacher reviews the *igh* vowel team. Students use letter tiles to add consonants to the vowel teams and to create words. As a review, students read aloud the list of words created.

Materials	Preparation
• Letter Tiles • Small box or a bag	• Cut out Letter Tiles. • Place consonant tiles in a small box or bag. (Reserve vowel team tiles for instruction.)

Teach Long i Vowel Teams

Ask: ***Who can tell me the sound for long* i*? (/ī/)*** Have students repeat /ī/.

Remind students: ***In a vowel team, letters work together to stand for the long vowel sound.***

Ask: ***Who can name a vowel team for the long i sound?***

Display the *igh* tile and elaborate: **Igh *is a long* i *vowel team. The letters* i, g, *and* h *work together to make the long sound /ī/.*** Have students repeat the long *I* sound.

Practice and Apply

Demonstrate: Place the *igh* tile on the table and say: ***Let's add letters to the long* i *team to make words. In this bag I have some letter tiles. These letters are consonants. I will draw two letters from the bag and add them to* igh *to see if I can make a word***

Have students draw tiles and create words. Guide them as needed. For example: ***Is that a word? Let's sound it out.*** Sweep your finger under the word. **/l/ /ī/ /t/ ... light. *Is it a word?*** Write the word on the whiteboard and have students repeat it with you.

Continue the activity. Have students draw new tiles and create new words. Replace tiles in bag as needed. As words are completed, write them on the whiteboard and have students repeat them with you.

Check Progress

Observe each student during practice and use the following activity to check progress made on the target skill. If student can read a word from each team, consider the intervention successful.

Display the list of words you have created. Explain: ***I will name a vowel team. Look at the list to find and read out loud one word with that vowel team.*** Demonstrate the task using a sample word from the list on the board. Alternate between vowel teams, giving each student several opportunities to read words.

igh	f	l	h
m	n	r	s
b	t	h	m
t	n	f	t

Reteaching Lessons

Words with oa and ow

Grade 1

15 min.

CCSS.RF.K.3b
TEKS 110.11.3.B

LEARNING OBJECTIVE: Decode words using the long *o* sound formed with the vowel teams *oa* and *ow*.

LANGUAGE OBJECTIVE: Use phonics clues to sound out words using the long *o* sound formed with the vowel teams *oa* and *ow*.

Lesson Overview

Teacher reviews the *oa* and *ow* vowel teams. Students use letter tiles to add consonants to the vowel teams and to create words. As a review, students read aloud the list of words created.

Materials	Preparation
• Letter Tiles • Small box or a bag	• Cut out Letter Tiles. • Place consonant tiles in a small box or bag. (Reserve vowel team tiles for instruction.)

Teach Long o Vowel Teams

Ask: ***Who can tell me the sound for long* o*? (/ō/)*** Have students repeat /ō/.

Remind students: ***In a vowel team, two letters work together to stand for the long vowel sound.***

Ask: ***Who can name one of the vowel teams for long* o *sound? Who can name the other vowel team?***

Display the *oa* tile and elaborate: ***oa is a long* o *vowel team. The letters* o *and* a *work together to make the long sound /ō/.*** Have students repeat the long *o* sound.

Display the *ow* tile and elaborate: ***ow is a long* o *vowel team. The letters* o *and* w *work together to make the long sound /ō/.*** Have students repeat the long *o* sound.

Practice and Apply

Demonstrate: ***Place the* oa *tile on the table and say: Let's add letters to the long* o *teams to make words. In this bag I have some letter tiles. These letters are consonants. I will draw two letters from the bag and add them to* oa *to see if I can make a word. I can add them before or after the vowel team.***

Have students draw tiles and create words. Guide them as needed. For example: ***Is that a word? Let's sound it out.*** Sweep your finger under the word. **/b/ /ō/ /t/ ... boat. *Is it a word?*** Write the word on the whiteboard and have students repeat it with you.

Continue the activity. Have students draw new tiles and create new words. Replace tiles in bag as needed. As words are completed, write them on the whiteboard and have students repeat them with you. After a few turns, challenge students to try adding a new tile to the last word created to see if they can make a five-letter word.

After students have created five or six words, change from *oa* to *ow*. Place the *ow* tile on the table. Have students draw new tiles and create new words. Replace tiles in bag as needed. As words are completed, write them on the whiteboard and have students repeat them with you.

After a few turns, challenge students to try adding a new tile to the last word created to see if they can make a five letter word. Write all words on the whiteboard and have students repeat them with you.

Check Progress

Observe each student during practice and use the following activity to check progress made on the target skill. If student can read a word from each team, consider the intervention successful.

Display the list of words you have created. Explain: ***I will name a vowel team. Look at the list to find and read out loud one word with that vowel team.*** Demonstrate the task using a sample word from the list on the board. Alternate between vowel teams, giving each student several opportunities to read words.

oa	ow	t	b
c	l	n	d
g	f	m	s
p	k	r	h

Reteaching Lessons ✓

Decodable Words

Words with ue, ew, and oo

Grade 1

15 min.

CCSS.RF.K.3b
TEKS 110.11.3.B

LEARNING OBJECTIVE: Decode words using the long *u* sound formed with the vowel teams *ue, ew,* and *oo.*

LANGUAGE OBJECTIVE: Use phonics clues to sound out words using the long *u* sound formed with the vowel teams *ue, ew,* and *oo.*

Lesson Overview

Teacher reviews the *ue* and *ew* vowel teams. Students use letter tiles to add consonants to the vowel teams and to create words. As a review, students read aloud the list of words created.

Materials	Preparation
• Letter Tiles • Small box or a bag	• Cut out Letter Tiles. • Place consonant tiles in a small box or bag. (Reserve vowel team tiles for instruction.)

Teach Long A Vowel Teams

Ask: ***Who can tell me the sound for long* u? (/ū/)** Have students repeat /ū/.

Remind students: ***In a vowel team, two letters work together to stand for the long vowel sound.***

Ask: ***Who can name one of the vowel teams for long u sound? Who can name the other vowel team?***

Display the *ue* tile and elaborate: **ue *is a long* u *vowel team. The letters* u *and* e *work together to make the long sound /ū/.*** Have students repeat the long *u* sound.

Display the *ew* tile and elaborate: **ew *is a long* u *vowel team. The letters* e *and* w *work together to make the long sound /ū/.*** Have students repeat the long *u* sound.

Display the *oo* tile and elaborate: **oo *is a long* u *vowel team. The letters* o *and* o *work together to make the long sound /ū/.*** Have students repeat the long *u* sound.

Practice and Apply

Demonstrate: Place the *ew* tile on the table and say: ***Let's add letters to the long* u *teams to make words. In this bag I have some letter tiles. These letters are consonants. I will draw two letter from the bag and add them to* ew *to see if I can make a word. I can add them before or after the vowel team.***

Have students draw tiles and create words. Guide them as needed. For example: ***Is that a word? Let's sound it out.*** Sweep your finger under the word. **/fl/ /ū/... flew. *Is it a word?*** Write the word on the whiteboard and have students repeat it with you.

Continue the activity. Have students draw new tiles and create new words. Replace tiles in bag as needed. As words are completed, write them on the whiteboard and have students repeat them with you.

After students have created five or six words, change the vowel team tile from *ew* to *ue* and then later from *ue* to *oo*.

For each vowel team, have students draw tiles and create new words. Replace tiles in bag as needed. Challenge students to try adding a new tile to the last word created to see if they can make longer words.

As words are completed, write them on the whiteboard and have students repeat them with you.

Check Progress

Observe each student during practice and use the following activity to check progress made on the target skill. If student can read a word from each team, consider the intervention successful.

Display the list of words you have created. Explain: ***I will name a vowel team. Look at the list to find and read out loud one word with that vowel team.*** Demonstrate the task using a sample word from the list on the board. Alternate between vowel teams, giving each student several opportunities to read words.

ue	ew	oo	s
t	r	d	c
h	g	l	n
k	f	w	m

Reteaching Lessons

Diphthongs oy and oi

Grade K

10 min.

CCSS.RF.2.3b
TEKS 110.13.2.A(iv)

LEARNING OBJECTIVE: Decode words formed with the vowel combinations (diphthongs) *oi* and *oy*.

LANGUAGE OBJECTIVE: Use phonics clues to read words and sentences containing *oi* and *oy*.

Lesson Overview

Teacher leads students to decode words formed with dipthongs *oi* and *oy*. Students then read decodable text containing words with *oi* and *oy*.

Materials	Preparation
• Silly Questions • Yes and No cards	• Cut Silly Questions into strips. • Cut out Yes and No cards.

NOTE: Silly Questions engage students in reading and decoding words in context. While the activity requires the student to respond, the answer is not the focus; students may express creative opinions. Use the Yes and No cards to keep all students engaged.

Teach and Model

Model the oy vowel combination. Write *boy* on the board. Ask: ***What's this word?*** Point to *oy* in *boy* and say: ***When the two vowels* o *and* y *are together in a word, they usually stand for the sound /oy/, as in* boy.** Have students repeat the word *boy*. Erase the *b* from *boy*. Point to *oy* and ask: ***What sound does this stand for?***

Repeat the process with *oi* using the word *coin*.

Model vowel-first blending. Write *toys* on the board. Point to *oy*.

Ask: ***What's this sound?*** Say: ***Now watch and listen as I read the word.*** Sweep your finger under the word and say: **toys**.

Say: ***Now you do it with me. When I point to the* oy*, say /oy/. When I move my finger under the word, say the whole word.*** Ask a volunteer to tell you the meaning of *toys* or to use it in a sentence.

Continue the process. Write words from the word bank on the board. Have students first say the vowel sound, then say the whole word, and then tell the meaning of the word or use it in a sentence.

Word bank for one-syllable words: joy, boys, soy, boil, point, choice, spoil, oil, soil, foil

Word bank for multisyllable words: enjoy, oyster, royal, loyal, pageboy, avoided, poison, noisy

Apply to decodable text: Silly Questions

Explain: ***Now that you can read words with* oi *and* oy*, you can read and answer some silly questions.***

Give each student a Yes card and a No card. Display a question and have one student read it out loud. Have all students respond to the question by placing their Yes or No card face down in front of them. Have students reveal their answers all at once. Allow one volunteer to explain his or her answer. Repeat with each silly question.

Check Progress

Observe each student during practice and use the following activity to check progress made on the target skill. If the student can correctly read two words, consider the intervention successful.

Write a word from the word bank on the board. Ask a student to identify the *oi* or *oy* pattern by pointing to it. Have the student read the word out loud.

One-syllable words: coy, ploy, soy, Roy, join, oil, soil, foil, void, moist, voice

Multisyllable words: annoy, deploy, busboy, destroy, boyish, joyful, voyage, foyer, coiling, avoid, pointing

Can Cowboy Roy ride an oyster?

Can you enjoy a new toy?

Can I buy soy with a coin made of foil?

Will a boy play in moist soil?

Should a royal king avoid his loyal pageboy?

Can a cook boil a pot of spoiled oil?

Reteaching Lessons ✓

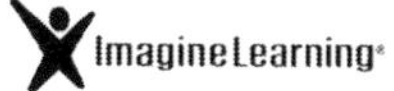

Yes

No

Yes

No

Yes

No

Yes

No

Yes

No

Diphthongs ow and ou

LEARNING OBJECTIVE: Decode words formed with the vowel combinations (diphthongs) *ow* and *ou*.

LANGUAGE OBJECTIVE: Use phonics clues to read words and sentences containing *ow* and *ou*.

Lesson Overview

Teacher leads students to decode words formed with dipthongs *ow* and *ou*. Students then read decodable text containing words with *ow* and *ou*.

Materials	Preparation
• Silly Questions • Yes and No cards	• Cut Silly Questions into strips. • Cut out Yes and No cards.

NOTE: Silly Questions engage students in reading and decoding words in context. While the activity requires the student to respond, the answer is not the focus; students may express creative opinions. Use the Yes and No cards to keep all students engaged.

Teach and Model

Model the *ow* vowel combination. Write *cow* on the board. Ask: ***What's this word?*** Point to *ow* in *cow* and say: ***When the two vowels* a *and* w *are together in a word, they usually stand for the sound /ow/, as in* cow.** Have students repeat the word *cow*. Erase the *c* from *cow*. Point to *ow* and ask: ***What sound does this stand for?***

Repeat the process with *ou* using the word *out*.

Model vowel-first blending. Write *down* on the board. Point to *oy*.

Ask: ***What's this sound?*** Say: ***Now watch and listen as I read the word.*** Sweep your finger under the word and say: **down**.

Say: ***Now you do it with me. When I point to the* ow*, say /ow/. When I move my finger under the word, say the whole word.*** Ask a volunteer to tell you the meaning of *down* or to use it in a sentence.

Continue the process. Write words from the word bank on the board. Have students first say the vowel sound, then say the whole word, and then tell the meaning of the word or use it in a sentence.

Word bank for one-syllable words: now, clown, brow, frown, howl, wow, found, foul, pouch, round, ouch

Word bank for multisyllable words: flower, allow, towel, chowder, time-out, doghouse, about, around, announce, cookout, counter

Apply to decodable text: Silly Questions

Explain: ***Now that you can read words with* ow *and* ou*, you can read and answer some silly questions.***

Give each student a Yes card and a No card. Display a question and have one student read it out loud. Have all students respond to the question by placing their Yes or No card face down in front of them. Have students reveal their answers all at once. Allow one volunteer to explain his or her answer. Repeat with each silly question.

Check Progress

Observe each student during practice and use the following activity to check progress made on the target skill. If the student can correctly read two words, consider the intervention successful.

Write a word from the word bank on the board. Ask a student to identify the *ow* or *ou* pattern by pointing to it. Have the student read the word out loud.

One-syllable words: proud, house, noun, mouth, bound, crowd, vow, prowl, owl, how, fowl, scowl

Multisyllable words: amount, pronounce, mountain, miscount, power, eyebrow, tower, county, vowel, download, powder

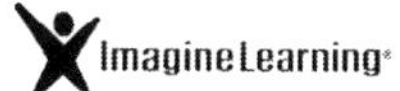

Can you wear a crown with a brown gown?

Can you ride downtown on a cow?

Does a cloud make a loud sound?

Can you bounce on a couch for an hour?

Can you pound the ground with a flower?

Can you count out loud on a mountain?

Yes

No

Yes

No

Yes

No

Yes

No

Yes

No

Decodable Words

Diphthongs aw and au

Grade K

10 min.

CCSS.RF.2.3b
TEKS 110.13.2.A(iv)

LEARNING OBJECTIVE: Decode words formed with the vowel combinations (diphthongs) *aw* and *au*.

LANGUAGE OBJECTIVE: Use phonics clues to read words and sentences containing *aw* and *au*.

Lesson Overview

Teacher leads students to decode words formed with dipthongs *aw* and *au*. Students then read decodable text containing words with *aw* and *au*.

Materials	Preparation
• Silly Questions • Yes and No cards	• Cut Silly Questions into strips. • Cut out Yes and No cards.

NOTE: Silly Questions engage students in reading and decoding words in context. While the activity requires the student to respond, the answer is not the focus; students may express creative opinions. Use the Yes and No cards to keep all students engaged.

Reteaching Lessons

Teach and Model

Model the *aw* vowel combination. Write *jaw* on the board. Ask: ***What's this word?*** Point to *aw* in *jaw* and say: ***When the two vowels* a *and* w *are together in a word, they usually stand for the sound /aw/, as in* jaw.** Have students repeat the word *jaw*. Erase the *j* from *jaw*. Point to *aw* and ask: ***What sound does this stand for?***

Repeat the process with *au* using the word *haul*.

Model vowel-first blending. Write *hawk* on the board. Point to *oy*.

Ask: ***What's this sound?*** Say: ***Now watch and listen as I read the word.*** Sweep your finger under the word and say: **hawk**.

Say: ***Now you do it with me. When I point to the* aw*, say /aw/. When I move my finger under the word, say the whole word.*** Ask a volunteer to tell you the meaning of *hawk* or to use it in a sentence.

Continue the process. Write words from the word bank on the board. Have students first say the vowel sound, then say the whole word, and then tell the meaning of the word or use it in a sentence.

Word bank for one-syllable words: crawl, law, draw, lawn, thaw, caught, cause, fault, sauce, pause, taught

Word bank for multisyllable words: awful, strawberry, sawdust, coleslaw, withdraw, caution, applaud, faucet, haunted, overhaul, laundry

Apply to decodable text: Silly Questions

Explain: ***Now that you can read words with* aw *and* au*, you can read and answer some silly questions.***

Give each student a Yes card and a No card. Display a question and have one student read it out loud. Have all students respond to the question by placing their Yes or No card face down in front of them. Have students reveal their answers all at once. Allow one volunteer to explain his or her answer. Repeat with each silly question.

Check Progress

Observe each student during practice and use the following activity to check progress made on the target skill. If the student can correctly read two words, consider the intervention successful.

Write a word from the word bank on the board. Ask a student to identify the *aw* or *au* pattern by pointing to it. Have the student read the word out loud.

One-syllable words: claw, yawn, dawn, paw, saw, jaw, flaw, shawl, faun, fraud, vault

Multisyllable words: flawless, bandsaw, awesome, awning, seesaw, jigsaw, daughter, autumn, bauble, cauldron, auction

Would you eat raw sausage with a straw?

Can you mow the lawn with a saw?

Can you make applesauce in August?

Will an exhausted author sign an autograph?

Can an astronaut launch in a rickshaw?

Will an awkward fawn crawl on a seesaw?

 Yes	 No
 Yes	 No
 Yes	 No
 Yes	 No
 Yes	 No

Decodable Words

Long oo, Short oo

Grades 1-2

15 min.

CCSS.RF.2.3b
TEKS 110.12.3.A(v)

LEARNING OBJECTIVE: Identify and decode words formed with the vowel digraph *oo*.
LANGUAGE OBJECTIVE: Read and sort words with vowel digraph *oo* and locate them in decodable text.

Lesson Overview

Teacher guides students to decode and sort long *oo* and short *oo* words. Students locate, circle, and read target words in two simple texts.

Materials	Preparation
• One-Syllable *oo* Word Cards • Two-Syllables *oo* Word Cards • Boot and Hook cards • Decodable Texts: *Who Did It, Good Luck*	• Cut out word cards. Keep one-syllable cards separate from two-syllable cards. • Cut out boot and hook cards. • Separate *spoon*, *look*, and *classroom* from the one syllable *oo* word cards.

Teach and Model

Display four word cards on the table: *boot*, *hoop*, *pool*, and *hook*.

Say: ***When two o's are together, words can look similar but be pronounced differently. Listen.*** Read the four words out loud, emphasizing the long *oo* or short *oo* digraph.

Ask: ***Which card does not belong?*** If needed, prompt students to recognize that *hook* has a short *oo* sound and the other three words each have a long *oo* sound.

Explain: ***The two o's together can stand for the sound* oo *as in* boot*, or* oo *as in* hook.**

Practice and Apply: One Syllable Word Sort

Place the one syllable *oo* cards face down in a stack.

Say: ***We're going to read words and decide if they have the long* oo *sound, as in* boot*, or the short* oo *sound, as in* hook.**

Display the *boot* image.

Say: ***When we read a word that has the long sound /ō͞o/, we will sort it into this* boot.**

Display the *hook* image.

Say: ***When we read a word that has the short sound /ŏo/, we will sort it onto this* hook.**

Model sorting the one-syllable words *hook* and *boot*. Draw the card *look* and say the word out loud.

Say: **Look *has the short sound so I will put it on the* hook.**

Draw the card *spoon* and say the word out loud.

Say: **Spoon *has the long sound so I will put it in the* boot.**

Have students select a card, read the word out loud, and sort it to the correct image.

One-Syllable oo *Word Cards (short oo; hook):* look, hood, crook, took, cook, good, foot, book, wood, stood

One-Syllable oo *Word Cards (long oo; boot):* spoon, tool, hoop, stool, pool, noon, loop, tooth, food, moon

Practice and Apply: Two Syllable Word Sort

Place the two syllable *oo* cards face down in a stack.

Say: ***Now we can use what we know to read longer words.***

Model reading the two-syllable word *classroom*. Draw the card *classroom* and say the word out loud.

Reteaching Lessons

Model thinking: ***I know this part of the word:* room*. It has the long vowel sound like* boot*. Knowing that can help me to read the whole word* classroom*. This word goes in the* boot.**

Have students select a card, read the word out loud, and sort it to the correct image.

Two Syllable oo *Word Cards (short oo; hook):* woodland, unhook, textbook, notebook, football, cookies, lookout, understood, wooden, woolen

Two Syllable oo *Word Cards (long oo; boot):* classroom, toothbrush, moonlight, toadstool, balloons, toolbox, tablespoon, booster, ballroom, drooping

Practice and Apply: Apply to Decodable Text

Give each pair of students a Decodable Text printout. Have pairs work together to circle words with long and short *oo*. Then have students read the words aloud with their partner.

*Who Did It?**

Cooper walked into his **room**. What a mess!
Someone had been in here. Who was it?
There were a few clues around the **room**.
That **looked** like a shoe print in a chunk of mud.
There was a clue by the chest **too**.
His blue **boot** was in a **pool** of glue.
Who had come into his **room**?
Who had made this mess?
Just then, **Scoop**, the cat, walked in with his shoe.
"I know who did this," said **Cooper**. "It was you."
"Mew," said **Scoop**.
**oo words are identified in bold*

*Good Luck**

There was a lock on the truck.
So the **crook** used a rock to get in.
Then he **took** a sack out of it.
He **shook** the sack. Yes! Money.
Then he **looked** back to see if anyone saw him.
Good luck. He was safe.
Just then, a big **hook** came down from the sky.
The **hook** got the **crook** and **took** him back to the truck.
He was stuck. He couldn't get away from the **hook**.
Soon they came and took the **crook** to jail.
And where did the **hook** come from?
Up here. We saw it all.
**oo words are identified in bold*

Check Progress

Observe each student during practice and use the following activity to check progress made on the target skill. If student can read two words correctly, consider the intervention successful.

Use a copy of the Decodable Text printout.

Say: ***As I read, I will stop and point to a word. You read the word that I point to.***

Alternate between students, giving each student several opportunities to read long and short *oo* words.

look	hood
crook	took
cook	good
foot	book
wood	stood
spoon	tool
hoop	stool
pool	noon
loop	tooth
food	moon

Reteaching Lessons

woodland	unhook
textbook	notebook
football	cookies
lookout	understood
wooden	woolen
classroom	toothbrush
moonlight	toadstool
balloons	toolbox
tablespoon	booster
ballroom	drooping

Two Syllable oo Word Cards

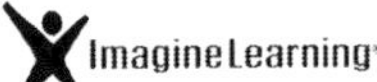

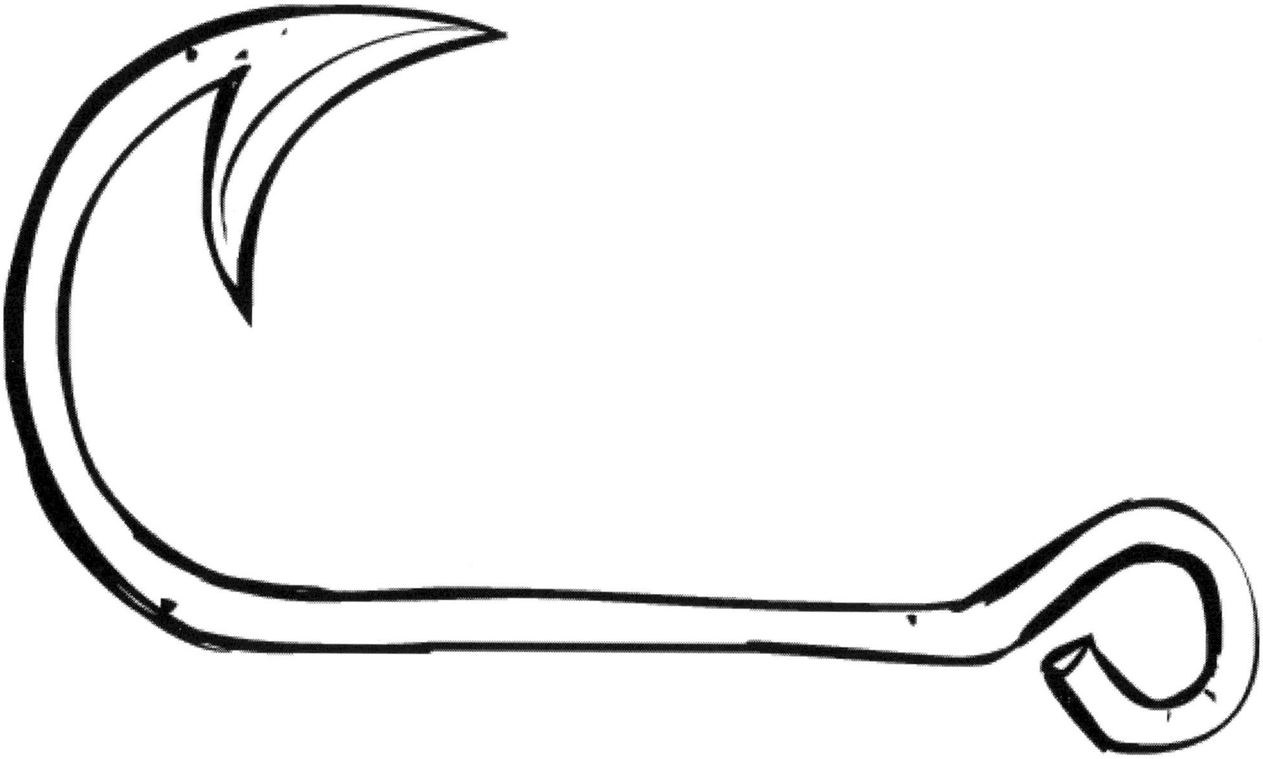

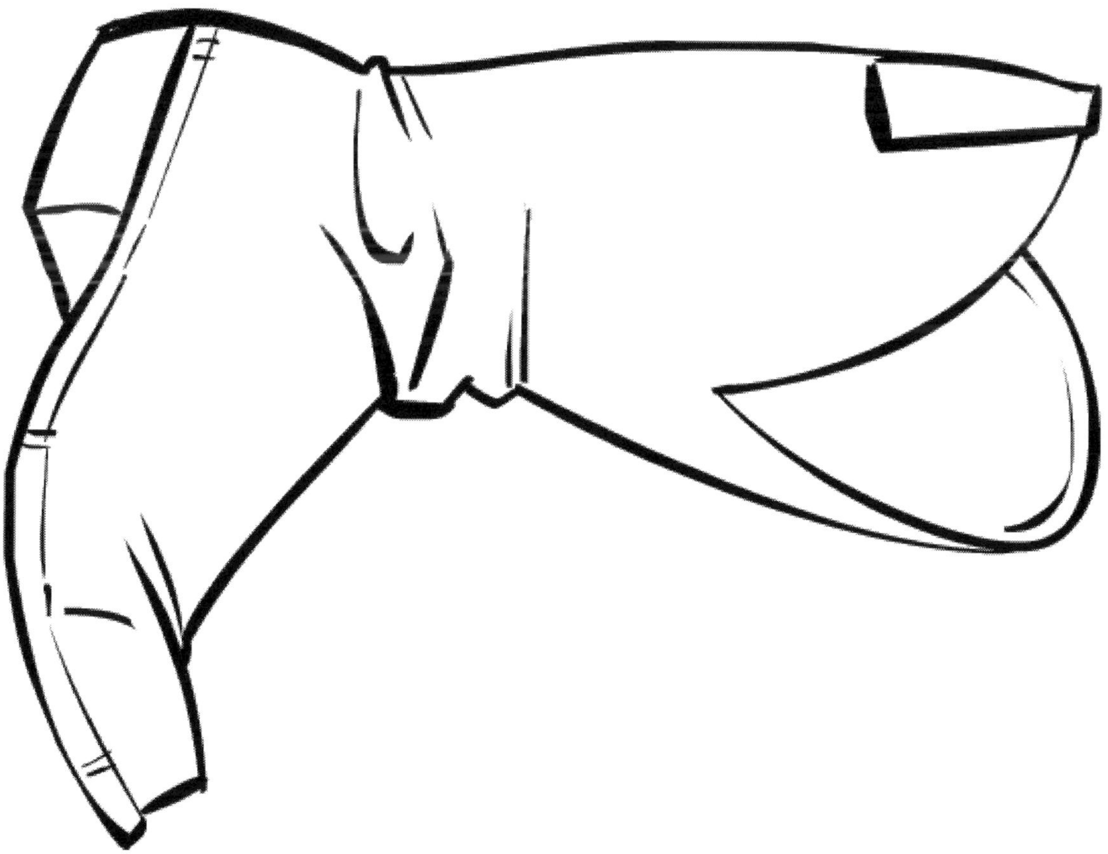

Who Did It?

Cooper walked into his room. What a mess!
Someone had been in here. Who was it?
There were a few clues around the room.
That looked like a shoe print in a chunk of mud.
There was a clue by the chest too.
His blue boot was in a pool of glue.
Who had come into his room?
Who had made this mess?
Just then, Scoop, the cat, walked in with his shoe.
"I know who did this," said Cooper. "It was you."
"Mew," said Scoop.

Good Luck

There was a lock on the truck.
So the crook used a rock to get in.
Then he took a sack out of it.
He shook the sack. Yes! Money.
Then he looked back to see if anyone saw him.
Good luck. He was safe.
Just then, a big hook came down from the sky.
The hook got the crook and took him back to the truck.
He was stuck. He couldn't get away from the hook.
Soon they came and took the crook to jail.
And where did the hook come from?
Up here. We saw it all.

Decodable Words

Ends with -nk or -ng

Grades 1–2

10 min.

CCSS.RF.2.3b
TEKS 110.12.3.A(v)

LEARNING OBJECTIVE: Recognize and decode words formed with the ending patterns *-ng* and *-nk*.

LANGUAGE OBJECTIVE: Use spelling patterns to write and sound out words ending in *-ng* and *-nk*.

Lesson Overview

Students match letter cards to create words that end in *-ng* and *-nk*. Students then read three words that end in *-ng*, or *-nk* and identify which of the three is not a real word.

Materials	Preparation
• Picture Cards • Word Cards • Word Strips	• Cut out word cards and separate beginning and ending cards. • Place the beginning sounds (*b, t, s, w, h, sk, tr, f, sw, r, l,* and *st*) from the word cards into a bag. • Set aside one of the two letter *h's* to use as a model. • Cut out word strips.

Teach and Model

Display Picture Cards face up on a table or board. Show the bag with beginning sound cards.

Say: ***In this bag are cards that have beginning sounds for words. Take a card from the bag and say the sound out loud.***

Have students take turns, pulling one card from the bag until all cards are distributed. Have students say the sound on their card as they take it from the bag.

Display the *ang* card. Say: ***This is /ang/. Say /ang/. You can find this pattern at the end of many words. Learning and recognizing common patterns can help you read.***

Place the */h/* beginning card next to the */ang/* card.

Explain: ***We can add /h/ to /ang/ to make a word: /h/ /ang/.* Hang. *The word* hang *goes with this picture.***

Display the hanging monkey picture card. Ask: ***What can a monkey do?*** Place the monkey picture card next to the word *hang* to prompt a response.

Show the students the other picture cards. Say: ***Let's make a new word to match one of these pictures. Who has a card that we can put at the beginning of /ang/? Which picture does it match?***

Prompt the student with the *f* card to match it with *ang*. Have the student blend the sounds out loud to say the word *fang* and then locate the picture.

Display a different ending card and help students match the beginning sounds with the correct endings to complete the following words:

-ang	-ing	-ong	-ank	-ink	-onk	-unk
hang	ring	long	bank	sink	honk	skunk
fang	wing	strong	tank	wink	bonk	trunk

Practice and Apply: Can't Fool Me!

Say: ***Let's play a game called Can't Fool Me! I will show you three words that end in* -nk *or* -ng. *Two of them are real words, and one of them is a nonsense word. You will read them and then vote on which one you think is not a real word.***

Display row A of the Word Strips. Have students read them silently, then ask a volunteer to read them out loud.

Reteaching Lessons

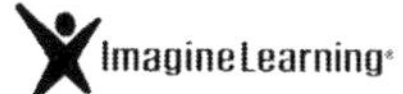

Say: ***Show me with your fingers. Which one is a nonsense word—one, two, or three?*** Have the students hold up one, two, or three fingers to show their choice. Give feedback on their choices. If any of the students have chosen a real word as a nonsense word, define it for them or use it in a sentence.

Say: ***Let's do more words. Now make your choice in secret. Keep your fingers under the table until I tell you to hold them up.***

Continue the same process for all of the Word Strips.

Nonsense Word Answer Key: A: blunk (2), B: thonk (3), C: sonk (1), D: stonk (2), E: strang (2), F: flong (3), G: sprong (1), H: lang (3)

Check Progress

Observe each student during practice and use the following activity to check progress made on the target skill. If the student can correctly read two words, consider the intervention successful.

Write a word from the word bank on the board and have a student read it. Continue until each student has had several opportunities.

Word Bank

Ends in -ng: sing, bang, song, ding, tang, tong, rang, rung, sling, clang, bring

Ends in -nk: link, bunk, wink, dunk, stink, chunk, brink, plank, clunk, clonk

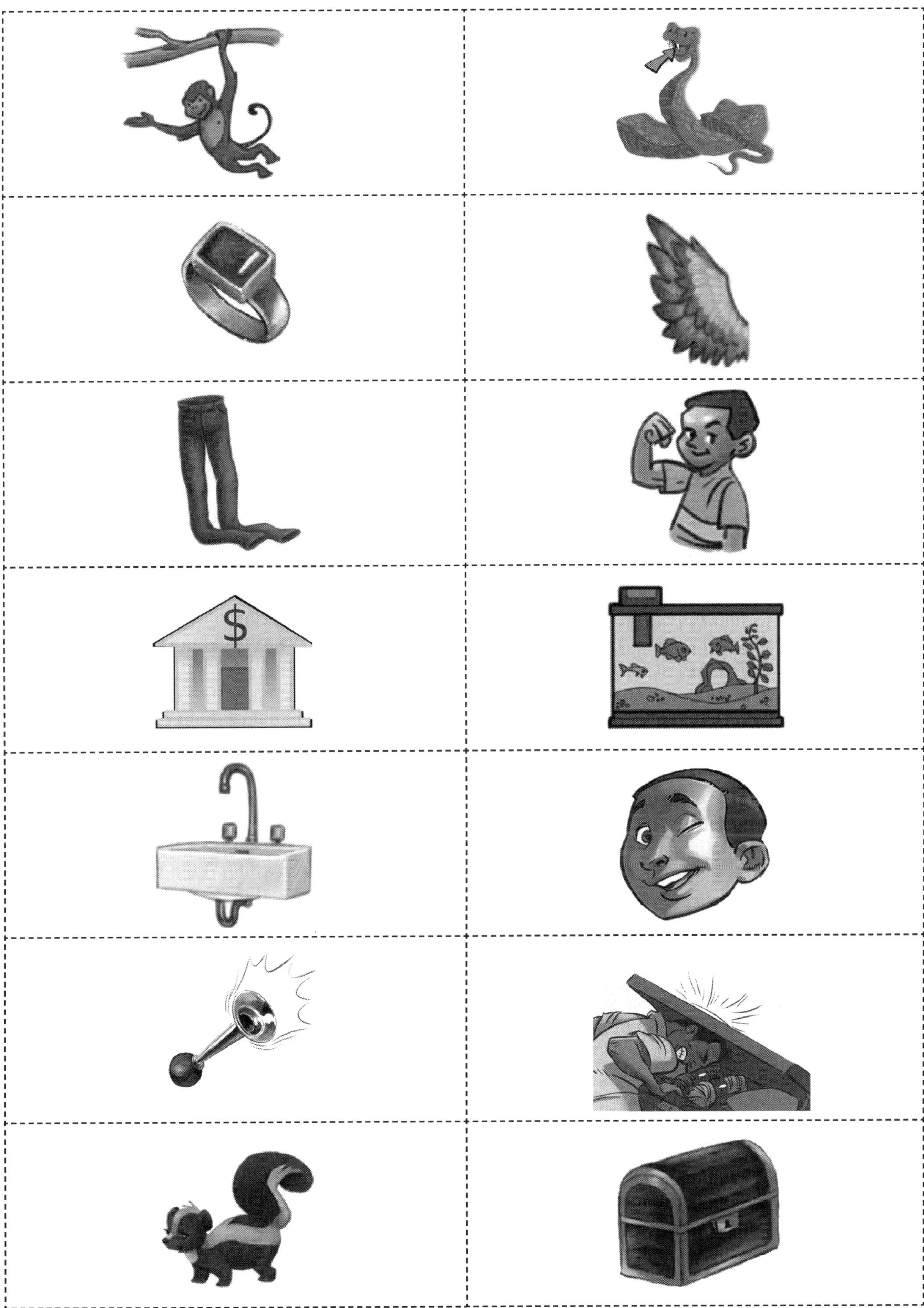

Reteaching Lessons

h ang	f ang
r ing	w ing
l ong	st rong
b ank	t ank
s ink	w ink
h onk	b onk
sk unk	tr unk

Reteaching Lessons

Word Cards

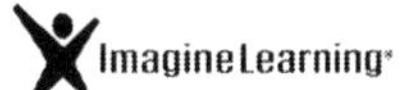

	1	2	3
A	blink	blunk	blank
B	think	thank	thonk
C	sonk	sunk	sink
D	stink	stonk	stunk
E	string	strang	strong
F	flung	fling	flong
G	sprong	spring	sprang
H	lung	long	lang

Decodable Words

ar, er, ir, or, ur

Grades 1–2

15 min.

CCSS.RF.1.3b
TEKS 110.12.3.C(vi)

LEARNING OBJECTIVE: Decode words formed with r-controlled vowels.
LANGUAGE OBJECTIVE: Produce the correct sound when reading words formed with r-controlled vowels.

Lesson Overview

Students recognize and decode words with r-controlled vowels (*ar*, *er*, *ir*, *or*, *ur*) and then apply skills by reading decodable text.

Materials	Preparation
• r-Controlled Word Chart • r-Controlled Word Strips • Decodable Text: *The Farm* (one per student pair)	• Cut out word strips along the dashed lines. • Fold each strip along the vertical dotted lines to hide the *r*.

Reteaching Lessons

Teach and Model

Explain: ***When* r *comes after a vowel, the vowel sound changes.***

Say, making the vowel sounds long and clear: ***Listen:* cat, cart*;* gill, girl.**

Explain: ***The* r *sound moves your mouth, and that changes the sound of the vowel.***

Model the changing sounds of *r*-controlled vowels. Display the Word Chart. Point to the letter *a*.

Say: ***When* r *comes after* a, a *changes to /ar/ as in* cart. *Say /ar/. Say* cart.**

Point to the letter *e*.

Say: ***When r comes after* e, e *changes to /er/ as in* her. *Say /er/. Say* her.**

Point to the letter *i*.

Say: **I *also changes to /er/ as in* girl. *Say /er/. Say girl.***

Point to the letter *u*.

Say: **U *also changes to /er/ as in* curl. *Say /er/. Say* curl.**

Point to the letter *o*.

Say: **O *can have two sounds.***

Point to the word *work*.

Say: **O *can change to /er/ as in* work. *Say /er/. Say* work.**

Point to the word *corn*.

Say: **O *can also change to /or/ as in corn. Say /or/. Say* corn.**

Display the folded word strip for *part* with the *r* hidden.

Ask: ***What's this word? Read it aloud with me two times:* pat, pat. *Now watch as we add an* r *after the vowel.***

Extend the fold of the word strip.

Ask: ***What's this word? Read it aloud with me two times:* part, part.**

Continue the process with remaining word strips. Each time, present the folded strip, direct students to say the word twice, and then unfold the strip and say the new word twice.

Practice and Apply

Apply words to decodable text.

Explain: ***Listen as I read a story. Listen for words that have a vowel followed by an* r.**

Read aloud *The Farm*. Then pair the students and provide each pair with a copy of *The Farm*.

Tell students to find and underline any words that have a vowel followed by an *r*. Monitor students as they work in pairs.

*The Farm**

Farmer **Bert works** hard.
He stops and looks out over his **farm**.
His **herd** of cows moos in the **yard**.
He hears the **birds** singing in the **birch** trees.
The **large** red **barn** shines in the sun.
Clouds **swirl** in the blue sky.
The corn stands tall and **firm**.
Fat pigs roll and **squirm** in the **dirt**.
Little chicks **chirp** and dig for **worms**.
Soft **ferns** sway in the **marsh**.
Rover runs and **barks** at the ducks.
But **Star** licks her **fur** and **purrs** softly.
Green vines and **flowers curl** on the fence.
The **cart** of hay **sparkles** like gold in the sun.
The **farm** is a **work** of **art**.

*Words with r-controlled vowels are bold

Say: ***Now, read the story quietly with your partner.***

Instruct students to whisper-read the story, alternating on each line. Monitor as they read and listen for errors. If necessary, pronounce non-decodable words for the students. After students read, summarize any common errors you have identified.

Check Progress

Observe each student during practice and use the following activity to check progress made on the target skill. If student can read two r*-controlled words correctly, consider the intervention successful.*

Have students read *The Farm*. Have each student read a line aloud, alternating until all have read several lines.

a	e i u	o
cart	her girl curl	work corn

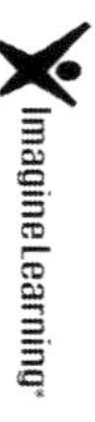

p	a	r	t
ch	a	r	t
b	e	r	g
b	i	r	d
w	o	r	k
sp	o	r	t
h	u	r	t
b	u	r	n

Reteaching Lessons ✓

The Farm

Farmer Bert works hard.
He stops and looks out over his farm.
His herd of cows moos in the yard.
He hears the birds singing in the birch trees.
The large red barn shines in the sun.
Clouds swirl in the blue sky.
The corn stands tall and firm.
Fat pigs roll and squirm in the dirt.
Little chicks chirp and dig for worms.
Soft ferns sway in the marsh.
Rover runs and barks at the ducks.
But Star licks her fur and purrs softly.
Green vines and flowers curl on the fence.
The cart of hay sparkles like gold in the sun.
The farm is a work of art.

Inflectional Endings

Grades 1–2
15 min.

CCSS.RF.1.3f
TEKS 110.12.3.E

LEARNING OBJECTIVE: Decode words formed with inflectional endings.
LANGUAGE OBJECTIVE: Divide words with inflectional endings into parts to sound them out.

Lesson Overview

Students separate words into parts to identify the suffix and determine the meaning. Using word cards, students play a game to build and decode words with the suffixes *ness*, *tion*, *ly*, and *ful*.

Materials	Preparation
• Inflectional Endings Example Cards • My Dog, Peaches Game Cards	• Cut out and fold example cards. • Cut out game cards.

Teach and Model

Explain: ***Sometimes we add letters to the end of base words to change their meaning. Knowing those endings can help you read. Let's look at six endings that you will see often when you read.***

Display all six example cards with the ending showing and the base words folded under.

Select and show the *s* card.

Say: ***This is the ending*** **s**. ***Watch and listen as I add*** **s** ***to a word. Flip over the folded word card to show*** **dog**.

Say: ***The base word is*** **dog.**

Open the card on the fold to add *s* to *dog*.

Say: ***When we add*** **s** ***to the end of*** **dog*****, it becomes a new word.*** Point to *dogs*.

Ask: ***What is the new word? How does adding*** **s** ***to the end of a base word change the meaning?***

If needed, prompt students to recognize that s changes the word to mean more than one.

Say: ***That's right. You can change a noun to show there is more than one by adding*** **s** ***to the end. For example: I have three dogs.***

Follow this process for the remaining word cards:

1. Display and say the ending.
2. Flip the card over. Display and say the base word.
3. Open the card to add the ending to the base word and say the whole word.
4. Ask a question to elicit understanding (i.e., ***What does [es] at the end of a word mean?***).
5. Summarize responses and give an example sentence for each ending as follows:

   -es: Sometimes you change nouns to show there is more than one by adding *es* to the end. For example: My dog eats peaches.

   -ing: Add *ing* to the end of a verb to show that the action is happening right now. For example: My dog is barking at a car.

   -ed: Add *ed* to the end of a verb to show that the action happened in the past. For example: My dog rolled in the mud.

   -er: Add *er* to the end of a word when you compare two things. It means *more*. For example: My dog is smaller than my friend's dog.

   -est: Add *est* to the end of a word when you compare more than two things. It means *most*. For example: My dog is the smartest of all the dogs.

Reteaching Lessons

Practice and Apply: My Dog, Peaches

Place game cards in a stack and make sure each student has a pencil.

Say: ***Let's play a game called My Dog, Peaches. In this game we'll read words with the endings we have just practiced. Then we'll use those words to make up sentences about our imaginary dog, Peaches.***

Instruct students to take turns drawing cards.

If the card shows a word, have students underline the base word and circle the ending. Then have students make up a sentence about Peaches, using the word on the card. If correct, the student keeps the card for one point.

If a student draws a "Peaches the dog" card, have the student take a card from another person in the group and make up a new sentence with that word. If correct, the student keeps the card.

Model the game for the students using the top card on the stack.

Check Progress

Observe each student during practice and use the following activity to check progress made on the target skill. If the student can correctly read two words, consider the intervention successful.

Write a word from the word bank and have a student circle the ending and read the word. Continue until each student has had several opportunities.

Word Bank:

-s: boys, bugs, hats, jobs, bees, clowns

-es: dresses, foxes, matches, brushes, kisses, bunches

-ed: helped, opened, rested, mashed, pointed, camped

-ing: pushing, looking, talking, singing, going, throwing

-er: sharper, older, longer, darker, lighter, sicker

-est: tallest, deepest, clearest, smartest, wildest, sweetest

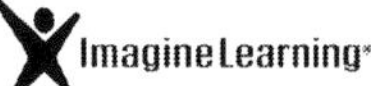

dog s 

peach es 

bark ing 

roll ed 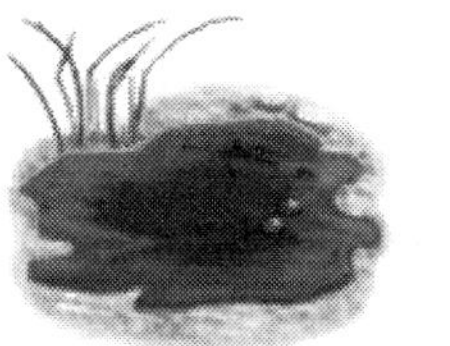

small er 

smart est 

Reteaching Lessons

flowers	toys
boxes	walked
licked	
messes	

Reteaching Lessons

sleeping

loudest

eating

cleanest

smarter

softer

Reteaching Lessons

cats	fastest
bushes	jumped
playing	
shorter	

Decodable Words

Suffixes

Grades 1–2

15 min.

CCSS.RF.2.3d
TEKS 110.12.2.D

LEARNING OBJECTIVE: Recognize and decode words formed with common suffixes *ness*, *tion*, *ly*, and *ful*.

LANGUAGE OBJECTIVE: Use strategies to sound out multisyllable words formed with the suffixes *ness*, *tion*, *ly*, and *ful*.

Lesson Overview

Students separate words into parts to identify the suffix and determine the meaning. Using word cards, students play a game to build and decode words with the suffixes *ness*, *tion*, *ly*, and *ful*.

Materials	Preparation
• Base Word Cards • Suffix Work Boards (one per student)	• Cut out Base Word Cards. • Cut out Suffix Work Boards.

Teach and Model

Write *colorful* on the board.

Say: ***When you see a word you don't understand, separate the word into parts. Let's separate this word.*** Draw a line to separate *color* into *color* and *ful*. Have students read the two word parts.

Say: ***Sometimes the word part at the end is a suffix. A suffix is a helpful word part to know because it changes the meaning of the base word.* Ful *is a suffix. Say the suffix* ful.**

Say: ***When you put* full *at the end of a base word, it changes the meaning.* Colorful *means* full of color.**

Write the words *hopeful* and *powerful* on the board.

Say: ***Look at these words. What do you see at the end of each one?*** Prompt students to identify *ful* at the end. Point to each word and have students say them with you.

Say: ***Now listen to these sentences:***

I am *hopeful* my team will win the game.
The *powerful* bulldozer pushed the pile of dirt.

Model the strategy. Write the word *helpful* on the board.

Say: ***Here is a strategy you can use to read words with suffixes.***

1. ***First, separate the suffix from the base word.*** Draw a line between *help* and *ful*.
2. ***Next, read the base word.*** Cover *ful* and have students say *help* with you.
3. ***Then, read the suffix and think about its meaning.*** Point to *ful* and have the students say it with you. Say: **Ful *means* full of.**
4. ***Finally, read the whole word.*** Sweep your finger under the whole word and have the students say it with you. Ask: ***What is the meaning of the whole word?***

Say: ***Let's try this with a new suffix.*** Repeat the process for the suffixes *ly*, *ness*, and *tion*.

Suffix	Meaning	Word bank	Sentence bank
-ly	shows a characteristic of something or how something is done	quickly, quietly, happily, loudly	The group of friends sat quietly together. The kitten played happily with the ball of string.
-ness	shows the quality of or condition of someone or something	kindness, neatness, sickness, weakness	We keep our desks clean because neatness is important. When we go on long trips, I have car sickness.

Reteaching Lessons

Suffix	Meaning	Word bank	Sentence bank
-(t)ion*	usually shows there is an action or process	action, subtraction, direction, attraction	I like to do subtraction problems in math. The map shows us the direction we need to go.

*Explain that often the suffix *tion* is shortened to *ion* when it is added to the base word.

Practice and Apply

Place Base Word Cards face down in a stack. Give each student a Suffix Work Board.

Have students select the top card from the stack and say the base word. Then have students place the word on their Suffix Work Board next to the suffix that makes a real word. Guide students as needed to find the correct suffix. (Note that some words will work with more than one suffix.) Finally, have the students say the whole word.

Base words: play, rude, elect, react, fit, quick, sudden, reflect, quest, select, great, stiff, shy, sharp, careful, perfect, silent, smooth, pain, fear, stress, thought, use, wonder

Possible words with ful*:* playful, fitful, painful, fearful, stressful, thoughtful, useful, wonderful

Possible words with ly*:* rudely, quickly, suddenly, stiffly, shyly, sharply, carefully, perfectly, silently, smoothly

Possible words with ness*:* rudeness, fitness, quickness, suddenness, greatness, stiffness, shyness, sharpness, carefulness, smoothness

Possible words with (t)ion*:* election, reaction, reflection, question, selection

Check Progress

Observe each student during practice and use the following activity to check progress made on the target skill. If the student can correctly read two words, consider the intervention successful.

Write a word from the word bank on the board. Have the student read the word out loud.

Word Bank: motion, pollution, goodness, darkness, illness, fitness, slowly, gladly, softly, sadly, thankful, careful, harmful, joyful

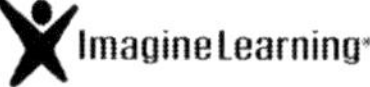

play	sudden
rude	reflect
elect	quest
react	select
fit	great
quick	stiff

Reteaching Lessons ✓

Reteaching Lessons

shy	sharp
careful	perfect
silent	smooth
pain	fear
stress	thought
use	wonder

	ful
	ly
	ness
	(t)ion

	ful
	ly
	ness
	(t)ion

Reteaching Lessons

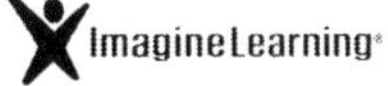

Prefixes

Grades 1–2

15 min.

CCSS.RF.2.3d
TEKS 110.12.2.D

LEARNING OBJECTIVE: Recognize and decode words formed with common prefixes *un* and *re*.
LANGUAGE OBJECTIVE: Use strategies to sound out multisyllable words formed with the prefixes *re* and *un*.

Lesson Overview

Students separate words into parts to identify the prefix and determine the meaning. Using word cards, students play a game to build and decode words with the prefixes *un* and *re*.

Materials	Preparation
• Base Word Cards • Prefix Work Boards (one per student)	• Cut out Base Word Cards. • Cut out Prefix Work Boards.

Teach and Model

Write *reuse* on the board.

Say: ***When you see a word you don't understand, separate the word into parts. Let's separate this word.*** Draw a line to separate *reuse* into *re* and *use*. Have students read the two word parts.

Say: ***Sometimes the first word part is a prefix. A prefix is a helpful word part to know because it changes the meaning of the base word.* Re *is a prefix. Say the prefix* re.**

Say: ***Each prefix has a special meaning.* Re *means* again. *When you put* re *before a base word, it changes the meaning. If you use something again, you reuse it.***

Write the words *rewrite*, *rethink*, and *replay* on the board.

Say: ***Look at these words. What do you see at the beginning of each one?*** Prompt students to identify *re* at the beginning. Point to each word and have students say them with you.

Say: ***Now listen to these sentences:***

> **We need more practice. The teacher asked us to *rewrite* the words.**
> **It is raining. We need to *rethink* our plans for recess.**
> **I really like that song. Can you *replay* it?**

Model the strategy. Write the word *rebuild* on the board.

Say: ***Here is a strategy you can use to read words with prefixes.***

1. ***First, separate the prefix from the base word.*** Draw a line between *re* and *build*.
2. ***Next, read the base word.*** Cover *re* and have students say *build* with you.
3. ***Then, read the prefix and think about its meaning.*** Point to *re* and have the students say it with you. Say: **Re *means* again.**
4. ***Finally, read the whole word.*** Sweep your finger under the whole word and have the students say it with you. Ask: ***What is the meaning of the whole word?***

Say: ***Let's try this with a new prefix.*** Repeat the process for the prefix *un*.

Prefix	Meaning	Word bank	Sentence bank
re-	again	rewrite, rethink, replay	We need more practice. The teacher asked us to *rewrite* the words. It is raining. We need to *rethink* our plans for recess. I really like that song. Can you *replay* it?
un-	not; opposite of	unfair, unhappy, unhurt, undo, unlucky	Max was *unhappy* when he heard his teacher was sick. Lisa slipped and fell but was *unhurt*. It is not too late to *undo* what I did.

Practice and Apply

Place Base Word Cards face down in a stack. Give each student a Prefix Work Board.

Have students select the top card from the stack and say the base word. Then have students place the word on their Prefix Work Board next to the prefix that makes a real word. Guide students as needed to find the correct prefix. (Note that some words will work with both prefixes.) Finally, have the students say the whole word.

Base words: able, take, true, fair, tied, do, invent, act, kind, build, lock, usual, write, direct, color, read

Possible words with re*:* retake, retied, redo, reinvent, react, rebuild, relock, rewrite, redirect, recolor, reread

Possible words with un*:* unable, untrue, unfair, untied, undo, unlock, unusual

Check Progress

Observe each student during practice and use the following activity to check progress made on the target skill. If the student can correctly read two words, consider the intervention successful.

Write a word from the word bank on the board. Have the student read the word out loud.

Word Bank: uncool, uncover, unpack, unclear, unready, unlike, uneven, reenter, reheat, remake, rename, repay, retell, refill

Extension Activity

Repeat the initial instruction for other common prefixes and create word cards for the practice game.

Prefix	Meaning	Word bank
im-	not	impossible, impatient, impolite
in-	not	inactive, incorrect, incomplete, invisible
over-	too much	oversleep, overdo, overeat, overhang
mis-	wrongly	misspell, misbehave, mislead, misread, misuse, mistreat
dis-	not; opposite of	discover, disagree, dislike, disappear, dishonest, distrust

able	kind
take	build
true	lock
fair	usual
tied	write
do	direct
invent	color
act	read

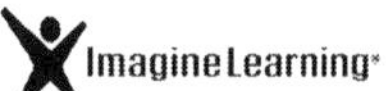

re	
un	

re	
un	

re	
un	

re	
un	

Reteaching Lessons

Decoding Multisyllabic Words

Grade 2

15 min.

CCSS.RF.2.3.C
TEKS 110.13.2.B

LEARNING OBJECTIVE: Identify long and short vowels in syllables and read two-syllable words.
LANGUAGE OBJECTIVE: Read syllables with long and short vowels and read two-syllable words.

Lesson Overview

Students identify vowels in a syllable as long or short and then read two-syllable words.

Materials	Preparation
• Syllable Vowel Demo Card • Column Header Cards • One-Syllable Flash Cards • Two-Syllable Flash Cards • Word Recognition Grid • Paper bag	• Cut out demo card and column header cards. • Cut out one-syllable flash cards. Set aside *pa*. • Cut out two-syllable flash cards. Set aside *fossil* and *robot*.

Teach and Model

Introduce the strategy of analyzing vowels in syllables.

Say: ***Every syllable has only one vowel sound. Look at this word.***

Display the Syllable Vowel Demo Card.

Ask: ***What is this word?*** Prompt students as needed.

Say: ***Yes, this one-syllable word is* bed*. The syllable has one vowel:* e*. To know what sound the vowel makes, look at the end of the syllable.***

Ask: ***Is* d *a consonant or vowel?*** Prompt students as needed.

Say: ***Right. The letter* d *is a consonant. When a syllable ends in a consonant, the vowel has a short vowel sound: /ĕ/.* Bed.** Point to the *e* in *bed*.

Say: ***Let's look at another word.*** Fold the demo word card to show the word *be*.

Ask: ***What is this word?*** Prompt students to say *be* as needed.

Say: ***Yes, this one-syllable word is* be*. Does this syllable end in a vowel or a consonant?*** Prompt students as needed.

Say: ***Yes, it ends in a vowel. When a syllable ends in a vowel, it has a long vowel sound: /ē/.* Be.** Point to the *e* in *be*.

Say: ***This letter stands for /ē/. Say this word again:* be.**

Practice and Apply: One-Syllable Sort

On the table, display column header cards *bed* and *be*. Allow enough space for a column of picture cards below the letter cards. Place the remaining one-syllable flash cards in a stack.

Introduce syllable sorting: ***Let's read some one-syllable word parts. Remember, if it ends in a consonant, the syllable has a short vowel sound. If it doesn't, it has a long vowel sound.***

Show the flash card *pa*.

Ask: ***Does this syllable end with a vowel or a consonant? Is the vowel long or short?*** Prompt students as needed.

Say: ***Right, the vowel sound is long. Let's read the syllable:* /pā/, /pā/.** Place the flash card *pa* in the column under *be*.

Say: ***Draw a flash card and read the syllable. Then sort the syllable into the correct column. If the syllable ends in a consonant, it has a short vowel and goes under* bed*. If the syllable ends in a long vowel, it goes under* be.**

Have students take turns reading and sorting syllable flash cards. Use the following prompts as needed: ***Does the syllable end with a vowel or a consonant? Is the vowel long or short? What is the vowel sound?***

After all syllable cards have been sorted into columns, point randomly to the flash cards and ask students to read each syllable

One-Syllable Flash Cards: pa (/pā/ as in *paper*), lim (/lĭm/ as in *limber*), sup (/sŭp/ as in *supper*), ri (/rī/ as in *rival*), ro (/rō/ as in *robot*), tam (/tăm/ as in *stamp*), dif (/dĭf/as in *different*), fen (/fĕn/ as in *fender*), mod (/mŏd/ as in *model*), re (/rē/ as in *replay*)

Practice and Apply: Two-Syllable Grab Bag

Introduce the ideas of looking for vowels in a two-syllable word: ***We can do the same thing with two-syllable words. When we read a word with more than one syllable, we look at the vowels to break the word into syllables.***

Show the flash card *fos-sil.*

Ask: ***What vowels are in this word?*** Prompt students as needed to say *o* and *i.*

Point to the first syllable.

Say: ***Let's look at the first syllable,* f-o-s. *Does it have a long or short vowel?***

Say: ***Right, because there is a consonant at the end of the syllable it has a short vowel sound, /ŏ/. Let's sound it out: /fŏs/.***

Point to the second syllable.

Say: ***Look at the second syllable,* s-i-l. *Does it have a long or short vowel?***

Say: ***Right, the second syllable has a short vowel. Sound it out: /sĭl/.***

Sweep your finger under the whole word and read it with students.

Say: ***Read the whole word: /fŏs/-/sĭl/.* Fossil.**

Show the flash card *ro-bot.*

Ask: ***What are the vowels in this word?***

Say: ***Right, this word has two* o*'s. When I break it into syllables, I see the first syllable ends in* o*, so it is a long* o.**

Point to the first syllable and read it with students.

Say: ***Sound it out: /rō/.***

Ask: ***Does the second syllable have a long or short vowel?***

Say: ***Yes, the* t *makes the* o *a short vowel.*** Point to the second syllable and read it with students. ***Sound it out: /bŏt/.***

Sweep your finger under the whole word and read it with students.

Say: ***Read the whole word: /rō/ /bŏt/.* Robot.**

Introduce the game.

Say: ***Put all the flash cards in the bag. Now we will read two-syllable words. Take a card out of the bag, read each syllable, and then read the whole word.***

Students read two-syllable flash cards until every student has had several opportunities to read. Students keep the flash cards they can read and put the others back in the bag.

If needed, cover one syllable to help students sound out a syllable at a time. Note that vowels in unstressed syllables may make the schwa sound instead of the short vowel sound.

Two-Syllable Flash Cards: minus (mi•nus), robot (ro•bot), dentist (den•tist), restart (re•start), fever (fe•ver), plastic (plas•tic), absent (ab•sent), exit (ex•it), admit (ad•mit), upset (up•set), even (e•ven), total (to•tal), fossil (fos•sil), wisdom (wis•dom), contest (con•test), basket (bas•ket), focus (fo•cus), label (la•bel), human (hu•man), napkin (nap•kin)

Check Progress

Observe each student during practice and use the following activity to check progress made on the target skill. If the student can read two words, consider the intervention successful.

Show students the word recognition grid. Direct students to read aloud as you randomly point to each word. If the student does not read the word correctly the first time, point out where the syllable break is. Continue until each student has had several opportunities to read.

Word bank: minus, robot, dentist, restart, fever, plastic, absent, exit, admit, upset, even, total, fossil, wisdom, contest, basket, focus, label, human, napkin

Reteaching Lessons

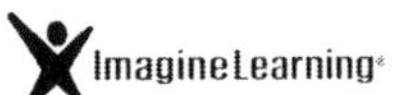

d

e

b

bed

be

ImagineLearning

pa	lim
sup	ri
ro	tam
dif	fen
mod	re

Reteaching Lessons

mi•nus minus	ro•bot robot
den•tist dentist	re•start restart
fe•ver fever	plas•tic plastic
ab•sent absent	ex•it exit
ad•mit admit	up•set upset

e•ven even	to•tal total
fos•sil fossil	wis•dom wisdom
con•test contest	bas•ket basket
fo•cus focus	la•bel label
hu•man human	nap•kin napkin

minus	robot
dentist	restart
fever	plastic
absent	exit
admit	upset
even	total
fossil	wisdom
contest	basket
focus	label
human	napkin

Long a Teams in Multisyllable Words

Grade 1

10 min.

CCSS.RF.1.3e
TEKS 110.12.3.A(v)

LEARNING OBJECTIVE: Decode and read advanced vocabulary words by analogy.
LANGUAGE OBJECTIVE: Use known words and patterns to sound out words formed with vowel teams.

Lesson Overview

Students decode and sort multisyllable words by focusing on vowel teams and breaking the word into parts.

Materials	Preparation
• Long a Chart printout • Word Cards • Small bag	• Cut out word cards. Set aside *painter*, *replay*, *skated*, *painful*, *delaying*, and *shaded*. • Place the remaining word cards in a bag.

Teach and Model

Ask: ***Who can tell me the sound for long* a*? Say it with me: /ā/.***

Display the Long a Chart.

Say: ***Here are three ways to spell the sound /ā/:* ai, ay, *and* a *with silent* e.**

Demonstrate word sorting: ***When you see these patterns in a word, you know there is a long* a *sound. Here are three examples.*** Point to the clue words *paint*, *play*, and *skate*.

Have students read each word with you. Ask a volunteer to underline the long *a* pattern in each word. Repeat each word one more time.

Explain: ***We can use what we know about these words to help us read. When you see a long word, you can break it into parts. Sometimes the parts of a longer word are the same as a word you already know.***

Display the word *painter*. Have a volunteer underline the vowel team.

Say: ***Say this word with me in two parts:* paint-er. *Now ask yourself: "When I look at each part, do I see any words I know?"*** If needed, use masking to prompt students to identify the word *paint*.

Say: ***Let's add this word to a column on our chart. Which pattern does this word use for the long* a *sound?*** Have a volunteer add the card to the *ai* column.

Repeat the process with the words *replay* and *skated*, adding each word card to the column with the corresponding vowel sound.

Explain: ***Sometimes you will see parts in longer words that are not the same, but that are similar. That can also help you. You know that the word* paint *has the sound* -ain. *You can use that to help you read longer words like* fainted *or* explaining.**

Display the word *painful*. Have a volunteer underline the vowel team.

Say: ***Say this word with me in two parts:* pain-ful. *Ask yourself, "Do I know any other words that look and sound like this word?"*** If needed, prompt students to identify that *pain* is similar to *paint*. Then have a volunteer add the card to the *ai* column. Repeat with the words *delaying* and *shaded*, adding those word cards to their respective columns.

Practice and Apply

Show the bag of word cards.

Say: ***There are many more words with the long* a *sound. Let's sort these words.***

Draw a card from the bag. Model the activity and establish the steps for students to follow: ***Look at each word card and underline the letters that stand for the long* a *sound.***

Continue modeling: ***Read the word quietly and break it into parts. Ask yourself, "What do the words I know tell me about this word?" Sound out the word until you can read it quickly and smoothly. Be ready to read it to the group and put it into the correct column.***

Reteaching Lessons

Have each student draw a card from the bag and guide them through this process. Then have students draw more cards from the bag until all words are distributed. Monitor students as they mark and sound out the remaining words.

Regroup. Have a volunteer show a card, read the word aloud, and then place the word card in the corresponding column. Continue until students have sorted each of their words.

Word Cards: painter, replay, skated, painful, delaying, shaded, display, awake, crayon, celebrate, container, yesterday, entertain, amaze, railroad, payable, motivated, fainted, decaying, lemonade

Check Progress

Observe each student during practice and use the following activity to check progress made on the target skill. If the student can read two words, consider the intervention successful.

Write a word from the word bank on the board and have a student read it. Continue until each student has had several opportunities.

Word Bank: gaining, sprayer, vibrated, explained, swaying, mistake, await, today, unsafe, rainy, played, educate

ai	ay	a_e

paint	play	skate

painter	replay	skated	painful
delaying	shaded	display	awake
crayon	celebrate	container	yesterday
entertain	amaze	railroad	payable
motivated	fainted	decaying	lemonade

Long e Teams in Multisyllable Words

LEARNING OBJECTIVE: Decode and read advanced vocabulary words by analogy.
LANGUAGE OBJECTIVE: Use known words and patterns to sound out words formed with vowel teams.

Lesson Overview

Students decode and sort multisyllable words by focusing on vowel teams and breaking the word into parts.

Materials	Preparation
• Long e Chart printout • Word Cards • Small bag	• Cut out word cards. Set aside *sleepless*, *eating*, *deepen*, and *treated*. • Place the remaining word cards in a bag.

Teach and Model

Ask: ***Who can tell me the sound for long* e*? Say it with me: /ē/.***

Display the Long e Chart.

Say: ***Here are two ways to spell the sound /ē/:* ea *and* ee.**

Demonstrate word sorting: ***When you see these patterns in a word, you know there is a long* e *sound. Here are two examples.*** Point to the clue words *sleep* and *eat*.

Have students read each word with you. Ask a volunteer to underline the long *e* pattern in each word. Repeat each word one more time.

Explain: ***We can use what we know about these words to help us read. When you see a long word, you can break it into parts. Sometimes the parts of a longer word are the same as a word you already know.***

Display the word *sleepless*. Have a volunteer underline the vowel team.

Say: ***Say this word with me in two parts:* sleep-less. *Now ask yourself: "When I look at each part, do I see any words I know?"*** If needed, use masking to prompt students to identify the word *sleep*.

Say: ***Let's add this word to a column on our chart. Which pattern does this word use for the long* e *sound?*** Have a volunteer add the card to the *ee* column.

Repeat the process with the word *eating*, adding the word card to the column with the *ea* vowel sound.

Explain: ***Sometimes you will see parts in longer words that are not the same, but that are similar. That can also help you. You know that the word* sleep *has the sound* -eep. *You can use that to help you read longer words like* keeper *or* sweeping.**

Display the word *deepen*. Have a volunteer underline the vowel team.

Say: ***Say this word with me in two parts:* deep-en. *Ask yourself, "Do I know any other words that look and sound like this word?"*** If needed, prompt students to identify that *deep* is similar to *sleep*. Then have a volunteer add the card to the *ee* column. Repeat with the word *treated*, adding it to the *ea* column.

Practice and Apply

Show the bag of word cards.

Say: ***There are many more words with the long* e *sound. Let's sort these words.***

Draw a card from the bag. Model the activity and establish the steps for students to follow: ***Look at each word card and underline the letters that stand for the long* e *sound.***

Continue modeling: ***Read the word quietly and break it into parts. Ask yourself, "What do the words I know tell me about this word?" Sound out the word until you can read it quickly and smoothly. Be ready to read it to the group and put it into the correct column.***

Have each student draw a card from the bag and guide them through this process. Then have students draw more cards from the bag until all words are distributed. Monitor students as they mark and sound out the remaining words.

Regroup. Have a volunteer show a card, read the word aloud, and then place the word card in the corresponding column. Continue until students have sorted each of their words.

Word Cards: sleepless, eating, deepen, treated, leaders, leaking, cleaner, misleading, overheat, season, peeking, freedom, freezer, speechless, seeing, agreement, meeting, creamy, cheaper, squeaky

Check Progress

Observe each student during practice and use the following activity to check progress made on the target skill. If the student can read two words, consider the intervention successful.

Write a word from the word bank on the board and have a student read it. Continue until each student has had several opportunities.

Word Bank: eager, heater, speaker, mistreat, unbeatable, leaking, streams, steamed, indeed, sweetener, sleepy, speedy, between, beetles

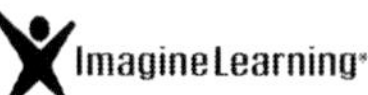

ee	ea

sleep	eat

sleepless	eating	deepen	treated
leaders	leaking	cleaner	misleading
overheat	season	peeking	freedom
freezer	speechless	seeing	agreement
meeting	creamy	cheaper	squeaky

Long i Teams in Multisyllable Words

Grade 1

10 min.

CCSS.RF.1.3e
TEKS 110.12.3.A(v)

LEARNING OBJECTIVE: Decode and read advanced vocabulary words by analogy.
LANGUAGE OBJECTIVE: Use known words and patterns to sound out words formed with vowel teams.

Lesson Overview

Students decode and sort multisyllable words by focusing on vowel teams and breaking the word into parts.

Materials	Preparation
• Long i Chart printout • Word Cards • Small bag	• Cut out word cards. Set aside *motorbike*, *lightning*, *unlike*, and *brightly*. • Place the remaining word cards in a bag.

Teach and Model

Ask: ***Who can tell me the sound for long* i*? Say it with me: /ī/.***

Display the Long i Chart.

Say: ***Here are two ways to spell the sound /ī/:* igh *and* i *with silent* e.**

Demonstrate word sorting: ***When you see these patterns in a word, you know there is a long* i *sound. Here are two examples.*** Point to the clue words *bike* and *light*.

Have students read each word with you. Ask a volunteer to underline the long *i* pattern in each word. Repeat each word one more time.

Explain: ***We can use what we know about these words to help us read. When you see a long word, you can break it into parts. Sometimes the parts of a longer word are the same as a word you already know.***

Display the word *motorbike*. Have a volunteer underline the vowel team.

Say: ***Say this word with me in two parts:* motor-bike. *Now ask yourself: "When I look at each part, do I see any words I know?"*** If needed, use masking to prompt students to identify the word *motor*.

Say: ***Let's add this word to a column on our chart. Which pattern does this word use for the long* i *sound?*** Have a volunteer add the card to the *i_e* column.

Repeat the process with the word *lightning* adding the word card to the column with the *igh* vowel sound.

Explain: ***Sometimes you will see parts in longer words that are not the same, but that are similar. That can also help you. You know that the word* bike *has the sound* -ike. *You can use that to help you read longer words like* hiker *or* lifelike.**

Display the word *unlike*. Have a volunteer underline the vowel team.

Say: ***Say this word with me in two parts:* un-like. *Ask yourself, "Do I know any other words that look and sound like this word?"*** If needed, prompt students to identify that *like* is similar to *bike*. Then have a volunteer add the card to the *i_e* column. Repeat with the word *brightly*, adding it to the *igh* column.

Practice and Apply

Show the bag of word cards.

Say: ***There are many more words with the long* i *sound. Let's sort these words.***

Draw a card from the bag. Model the activity and establish the steps for students to follow: ***Look at each word card and underline the letters that stand for the long* i *sound.***

Continue modeling: ***Read the word quietly and break it into parts. Ask yourself, "What do the words I know tell me about this word?" Sound out the word until you can read it quickly and smoothly. Be ready to read it to the group and put it into the correct column.***

Have each student draw a card from the bag and guide them through this process. Then have students draw more cards from the bag until all words are distributed. Monitor students as they mark and sound out the remaining words.

Regroup. Have a volunteer show a card, read the word aloud, and then place the word card in the corresponding column. Continue until students have sorted each of their words.

Word Cards: motorbike, lightning, unlike, brightly, hiker, reunite, memorize, arrive, ripened, divide, overnight, daylight, tighter, mighty, highchair, fighting, lighter, highest, describe, polite

Check Progress

Observe each student during practice and use the following activity to check progress made on the target skill. If the student can read two words, consider the intervention successful.

Write a word from the word bank on the board and have a student read it. Continue until each student has had several opportunities.

Word Bank: unite, likely, spotlight, nicest, devices, overpriced, invited, revise, beehive, higher, brighten, tonight, frighten

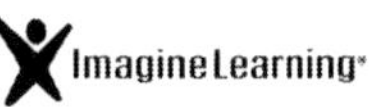

i_e	igh

bike	light

Reteaching Lessons

brightly	arrive	daylight	fighting	polite
unlike	memorize	overnight	highchair	describe
lightning	reunite	divide	mighty	highest
motorbike	hiker	ripened	tighter	lighter

Long o Teams in Multisyllable Words

Grade 1

10 min.

CCSS.RF.1.3e
TEKS 110.12.3.A(v)

LEARNING OBJECTIVE: Decode and read advanced vocabulary words by analogy.

LANGUAGE OBJECTIVE: Use known words and patterns to sound out words formed with vowel teams.

Lesson Overview

Students decode and sort multisyllable words by focusing on vowel teams and breaking the word into parts.

Materials	Preparation
• Long o Chart printout • Word Cards • Small bag	• Cut out word cards. Set aside *snowy*, *boating*, *golden*, and *microphone*. • Place the remaining word cards in a bag.

Teach and Model

Ask: ***Who can tell me the sound for long o? Say it with me: /ō/.***

Display the Long *o* Chart.

Say: ***Here are four spelling patterns that use the long o sound:* oa, ow, o *with silent* e, *and* old.**

Demonstrate word sorting: ***When you see these patterns in a word, you know there is a long o sound. Here are four examples.*** Point to the clue words *snowy*, *boating*, *golden*, and *microphone*.

Have students read each word with you. Ask a volunteer to underline the long *o* pattern in each word. Repeat each word one more time.

Explain: ***We can use what we know about these words to help us read. When you see a long word, you can break it into parts. Sometimes the parts of a longer word are the same as a word you already know.***

Display the word *snowy*. Have a volunteer underline the vowel team.

Say: ***Say this word with me in two parts:* snow-y. *Now ask yourself: "When I look at each part, do I see any words I know?"*** If needed, use masking to prompt students to identify the word *snow*.

Say: ***Let's add this word to a column on our chart. Which pattern does this word use for the long o sound?*** Have a volunteer add the card to the *ow* column.

Repeat the process with the words *boating*, *golden*, and *microphone*, adding each word card to the column with the corresponding vowel sound.

Explain: ***Sometimes you will see parts in longer words that are not the same, but that are similar. That can also help you. You know that the word* phone *has the sound* -one. *You can use that to help you read other long words like* backbone *or* postpone.**

Display the word *blowing*. Have a volunteer underline the vowel team.

Say: ***Say this word with me in two parts:* blow-ing. *Ask yourself, "Do I know any other words that look and sound like this word?"*** If needed, prompt students to identify that *blow* is similar to *snow*. Then have a volunteer add the card to the *ow* column. Repeat with the words *floated* and *retold*, adding those word cards to their respective columns.

Practice and Apply

Show the bag of word cards.

Say: ***There are many more words with the long o sound. Let's sort these words.***

Draw a card from the bag. Model the activity and establish the steps for students to follow: ***Look at each word card and underline the letters that stand for the long o sound.***

Continue modeling: ***Read the word quietly and break it into parts. Ask yourself, "What do the words I know tell me about this word?" Sound out the word until you can read it quickly and smoothly. Be ready to read it to the group and put it into the correct column.***

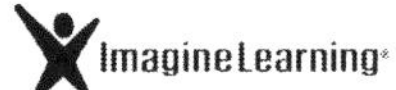

Have each student draw a card from the bag and guide them through this process. Then have students draw more cards from the bag until all words are distributed. Monitor students as they mark and sound out the remaining words.

Regroup. Have a volunteer show a card, read the word aloud, and then place the word card in the corresponding column. Continue until students have sorted each of their words.

Word Cards: snowy, boating, golden, microphone, blowing, floated, retold, backbone, envelope, coldest, moldy, rainbow, showing, lowest, unload, soaking, outspoken, foamy, followed, boldly

Check Progress

Observe each student during practice and use the following activity to check progress made on the target skill. If the student can read two words, consider the intervention successful.

Write a word from the word bank on the board and have a student read it. Continue until each student has had several opportunities.

Word Bank: holding, refolded, colder, frozen, spoken, reload, foaming, growing, shadow, slowly, oatmeal, broken, refolded, goldfish

o_e	ow	oa	old

phone	snow	boat	gold

snowy	boating	golden	microphone
blowing	floated	retold	backbone
envelope	coldest	moldy	rainbow
showing	lowest	unload	soaking
outspoken	foamy	followed	boldly

Long u Teams in Multisyllable Words

Grade 1

10 min.

CCSS.RF.1.3e
TEKS 110.12.3.A(v)

LEARNING OBJECTIVE: Decode and read advanced vocabulary words by analogy.
LANGUAGE OBJECTIVE: Use known words and patterns to sound out words formed with vowel teams.

Lesson Overview

Students decode and sort multisyllable words by focusing on vowel teams and breaking the word into parts.

Materials	Preparation
• Long u Chart printout • Word Cards • Small bag	• Cut out word cards. Set aside *jewelry*, *unglued*, and *tuneup*. • Place the remaining word cards in a bag.

Teach and Model

Ask: ***Who can tell me the sound for long* u*? Say it with me: /ū/.***

Display the Long u Chart. Say: ***Here are three ways to spell the sound /ū/:* ue, ew, *and* u *with silent* e.**

Demonstrate word sorting: ***When you see these patterns in a word, you know there is a long* u *sound. Here are three examples.*** Point to the clue words *glue*, *jewels*, and *tune*.

Have students read each word with you. Ask a volunteer to underline the long *u* pattern in each word. Repeat each word one more time.

Explain: ***We can use what we know about these words to help us read. When you see a long word, you can break it into parts. Sometimes the parts of a longer word are the same as a word you already know.***

Display the word *unglue*. Have a volunteer underline the vowel team.

Say: ***Say this word with me in two parts:* un-glue. *Now ask yourself: "When I look at each part, do I see any words I know?"*** If needed, use masking to prompt students to identify the prefix *un*.

Say: ***Let's add this word to a column on our chart. Which pattern does this word use for the long* u *sound?*** Have a volunteer add the card to the *ue* column.

Repeat the process with the words *jewelry* and *tuneup*, adding each word card to the column with the corresponding vowel sound.

Explain: ***Sometimes you will see parts in longer words that are not the same, but that are similar. That can also help you. You know that the word* glue *has the sound* -ue. *So, you can use that to help you read longer words like* immune *or* opportunity.**

Display the word *pruners*. Have a volunteer underline the vowel team.

Say: ***Say this word with me in two parts:* prun-ers. *Ask yourself, "Do I know any other words that look and sound like this word?"*** If needed, prompt students to identify that *prune* is similar to *tune*. Then have a volunteer add the card to the *u_e* column. Repeat with the words *rescued* and *chewing,* adding those word cards to their respective columns.

Practice and Apply

Show the bag of word cards.

Say: ***There are many more words with the long* u *sound. Let's sort these words.***

Draw a card from the bag. Model the activity and establish the steps for students to follow: ***Look at each word card and underline the letters that stand for the long* u *sound.***

Continue modeling: ***Read the word quietly and break it into parts. Ask yourself, "What do the words I know tell me about this word?" Sound out the word until you can read it quickly and smoothly. Be ready to read it to the group and put it into the correct column.***

Have each student draw a card from the bag and guide them through this process. Then have students draw more cards from the bag until all words are distributed. Monitor students as they mark and sound out the remaining words.

Regroup. Have a volunteer show a card, read the word aloud, and then place the word card in the corresponding column. Continue until students have sorted each of their words.

Word Cards: jewelry, tuneup, pruners, rescued, chewing, newspaper, screwdriver, dewdrop, interview, discontinue, Tuesday, attitude, overdue, blueberry, issue, attitude, perfume, refuel, introduce, tuneless

Check Progress

Observe each student during practice and use the following activity to check progress made on the target skill. If the student can read two words, consider the intervention successful.

Write a word from the word bank on the board and have a student read it. Continue until each student has had several opportunities.

Word Bank: unscrew, newest, jeweler, statue, tissue, untrue, continue, costume, computer, rudest

ue	ew	u_e

glue	jewels	tune

jewelry	tuneup	pruners	rescued
chewing	newspaper	screwdriver	dewdrop
interview	discontinue	Tuesday	attitude
overdue	blueberry	issue	attitude
perfume	refuel	introduce	tuneless

r-Controlled Multisyllable Words

Grades 1-2
15 min.

CCSS.RF.1.3e
TEKS 110.12.3.C(vi)

LEARNING OBJECTIVE: Decode multisyllable words formed with r-controlled vowels.
LANGUAGE OBJECTIVE: Use strategies to read multisyllable words formed with r-controlled vowels.

Lesson Overview

Students recognize and decode words with *r*-controlled vowels and then make and read words using syllable puzzle pieces.

Materials	Preparation
• Whiteboard and marker (one per student) • r-Controlled Puzzle Words • r-Controlled Word Cards	• Cut out puzzle word parts and place them in a bag.

NOTE: Whiteboards can be made with a piece of cardstock inserted in a plastic sheet protector. Use dry erase markers to write and tissues or small rags to erase. Many three-ring binders also have a clear plastic insert space on the front and back cover. These make a sturdier option that can be easily stored on a bookshelf.

Teach and Model

Introduce the letter combination *ar*. Write the letters *ar* on the board.

Say: ***The sound of these letters together is usually /ar/, as in cart. What sound is it?*** Have students repeat the */ar/* sound.

Explain: ***Listen to these words and see if you can hear /ar/ in these words. If you do, give me a thumbs up. If you don't, show me a thumbs down.***

Have students signal with their thumbs as you read these words (bold words have */ar/*): **marker**, pointed, **arches**, laundry, **hardly**, running, **sharpening**, **darken**.

Present a decoding strategy: ***The /ar/ sound is a part that you can find in many words. If you think about a word in parts, it can help you when you read big words.***

Say: ***I will say the parts of a word and then you say the whole word. Listen:* ar-ti-cle.** Say each syllable slowly, pausing between.

Ask: ***What word is it? Do you hear the /ar/ sound in article? Let's try a few more.*** Repeat the process with *farming (farm-ing)*, *backyard (back-yard)*, and *participate (par-ti-ci-pate)*.

Model spelling-focused blending. Write *parking* on the board and read it, pausing completely between word parts: **par-king.**

Ask: ***Where is /ar/ in this word?*** Have students point to *ar* and say */ar/*. Point to each part and have the students read the two parts aloud. Sweep your finger under the word and have the students repeat the whole word. Repeat the process with *departing (de-part-ing)*.

Connect decoding to spelling: ***I will write a word on the board. You say the parts of the word to yourself as you copy the word onto your board.*** Write the word *carpet* on the board. Have students copy it on their boards.

Ask: ***Do you see* ar *in this word? Circle it on your board. Let's read the word together. First, one part at a time, then the whole word.*** Point to and say each part of the word, pausing between parts. Then sweep your finger under the whole word and have student repeat it with you. Repeat with *marble (mar-ble)*, *safari (sa-fa-ri)*, and *apartment (a-part-ment)*.

Practice and Apply

Introduce the activity: ***Let's use puzzles to put word parts together into whole words.***

Have a student pull a puzzle piece from the bag and read the syllable. Do this with each student until all the pieces are distributed.

Ask one student to place a puzzle piece on the table.

Have all students look at the number on the puzzle piece and find any pieces they have with the same number, then join the pieces together to form a word.

Instruct the student who placed the first piece to lead the other students in the decoding strategy.

Say: ***Now you lead us in reading the word. First point to each puzzle piece and have us say each part of the word. Then sweep your finger under the word and have us read the whole word.***

Have students continue until all puzzle words have been completed.

r-*Controlled Puzzle Cards:* artistic, starting, harvested, arching, sharpener, marches, particles, target

Check Progress

Observe each student during practice and use the following activity to check progress made on the target skill. If a student can correctly read two words with r-controlled vowels, consider the intervention successful.

Show a student a word card. Have the student read the word out loud. Repeat until each student has had multiple chances to read a card.

r-*Controlled Word Cards:* smartest, pardon, discard, hardly, startle, sparkle, harden, farthest, darted, margin, unmarked, carpeted, carnival, scarlet, gardener, barnyard, armadillo, remarkable, carpenter, departed

1 ar	1 tist	1 ic	2 start	2 ing
3 har	3 vest	3 ed	4 arch	4 ing
5 shar	5 pen	5 er	6 march	6 es
8 par	8 ti	8 cles	7 tar	7 get

Reteaching Lessons

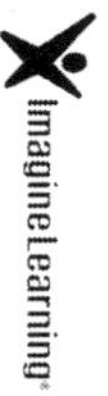

Reteaching Lessons

smartest	unmarked
pardon	carpeted
discard	carnival
hardly	scarlet
startle	gardener
sparkle	barnyard
harden	armadillo
farthest	remarkable
darted	carpenter
margin	departed

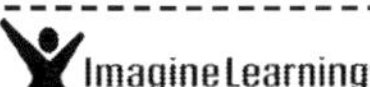

Notes

Reteaching Lessons

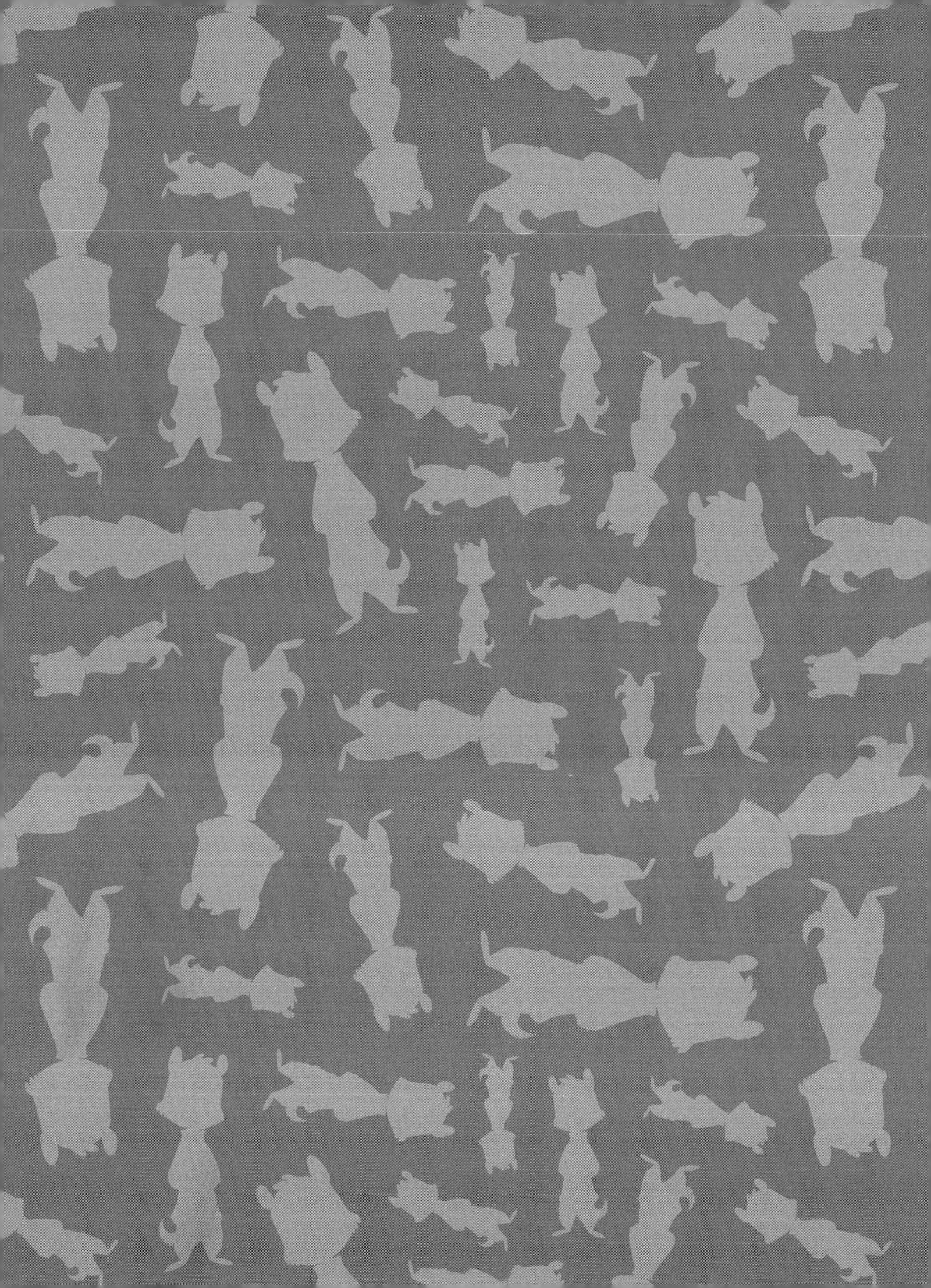

SIGHT WORDS

RETEACHING LESSONS

Developed with research-based methods, these instructional routines provide step-by-step instruction for dynamic activities that help students recognize and practice the most frequently occurring sight words. Each routine can be used for small group intervention and skill review or adapted for whole-class use. Also included in this section is a list of words from the Fry Word List that are included in Imagine Learning online curriculum. Listed with each Imagine Learning sight word is a decodable text that can be used to introduce and practice the word.

Analyze data in the Imagine Learning Action Areas Tool to identify groups of students who struggle with sight words, and use the Reteaching Lessons to provide additional support.

- Complete lesson plans that include modeling, practice, and assessment
- Interactive tasks to engage students and increase opportunities for successful learning
- Flexible routine format allows for use with any new or challenging words, based on student needs

Progress Tracking Sheet

Date	Student Name	Lesson/Skill	Intervention Successful (Y/N)	Notes

Progress Tracking Sheet

Date	Student Name	Lesson/Skill	Intervention Successful (Y/N)	Notes

Notes

Imagine Learning Sight Words List

Sight Words 1-50*			
Sight Word	**Imagine Learning Beginning Book (First Occurrence)**	**Sight Word**	**Imagine Learning Beginning Book (First Occurrence)**
a	*Too Hot*	one	*Not Mice!*
and	*Sam and Dad*	or	*Do Not Tap*
are	*Frog's Eggs*	said	*Wax Quiz*
as	*The Old Dog*	she	*Vote!*
be	*Oh the Pain!*	that	*Do Not Tap*
but	*Too Hot*	the	*Too Hot*
by	*Bob and the Bug*	their	*A Walk in the Dark*
can	*Do Not Tap*	there	*Not Mice!*
do	*Do Not Tap*	they	*The Band*
for	*Wax Quiz*	this	*The Map*
from	*Wax Quiz*	to	*Can You Come?*
have	*Pam's Hat*	was	*Vote!*
he	*Sam Is the Best*	we	*Do Not Tap*
his	*Sam Is the Best*	were	*Not Mice!*
I	*Where Am I?*	what	*Do Not Tap*
is	*Sam and Dad*	which	*A Walk in the Dark*
it	*Pam's Hat*	with	*Can You Come?*
not	*Sam and Dad*	you	*Too Hot*
of	*Let's Play Tag*	your	*Wax Quiz*

*Groupings based on the Fry Word List

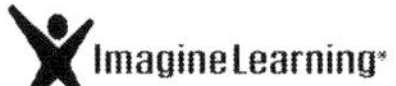

Sight Words 51–100			
Sight Word	**Imagine Learning Beginning Book (First Occurrence)**	**Sight Word**	**Imagine Learning Beginning Book (First Occurrence)**
about	*The Toy Robot*	no	*Stop, Bob, Stop!*
been	*Who Did It?*	now	*Sam and Dad*
come	*Can You Come?*	number	*Vote!*
could	*The Trunk of Money*	other	*Let's Play Tag*
down	*Stop That!*	out	*Good Luck*
first	*The Plane Race*	people	*A Walk in the Dark*
get	*Too Hot*	see	*Frog's Eggs*
go	*Too Hot*	so	*What a Bike!*
has	*Pam's Hat*	some	*Not Mice!*
her	*The Plane Race*	them	*Frog's Eggs*
him	*Good Luck*	then	*Stop, Bob, Stop!*
into	*The Frog*	these	*Not Mice!*
like	*Can You Come?*	two	*The Trunk of Money*
look	*The Map*	water	*Faster*
make	*Wax Quiz*	way	*The Plane Race*
many	*Bees*	who	*Who Did It?*
more	*The Clown*	will	*Can you Come?*
my	*What a Bike!*	would	*The Old Dog*

*Groupings based on the Fry Word List

Sight Words 101–200

Sight Word	Imagine Learning Beginning Book (First Occurrence)	Sight Word	Imagine Learning Beginning Book (First Occurrence)
after	*The Trunk of Money*	me	*Let's Play Tag*
again	*Sam Is the Best*	mother	*Sick and Bored*
air	*The Clown*	move	*First Place*
another	*A Walk in the Dark*	need	*Stop That!*
any	*The Toy Robot*	new	*Pam's Hat*
around	*The Frog*	off	*Crash!*
away	*Not Mice!*	our	*The Plane Race*
back	*Bob and the Bug*	over	*Oh the Pain!*
because	*The Scarecrow*	play	*I Want to Rest*
before	*The Trunk of Money*	put	*Where Are the Keys?*
boy	*The Old Dog*	should	*The Scarecrow*
does	*The New Rug*	take	*Wax Quiz*
even	*Sick and Bored*	too	*Stop, Bob, Stop!*
found	*The Map*	turn	*The Scarecrow*
give	*The Trunk of Money*	us	*Too Hot*
good	*Sam and Dad*	very	*The Old Dog*
here	*Where Am I?*	want	*Can You Come?*
house	*Run!*	where	*Where Am I?*
know	*Who Did it?*	work	*The Plane Race*

*Groupings based on the Fry Word List

Sight Words 201+			
Sight Word	**Imagine Learning Beginning Book (First Occurrence)**	**Sight Word**	**Imagine Learning Beginning Book (First Occurrence)**
across	*A Walk in the Dark*	let's	*The Map*
afraid	*Bees*	money	*Good Luck*
against	*The Car Wreck*	moon	*What a Bike!*
always	*Where Are the Keys?*	never	*I Want to Rest*
baby	*Frog's Eggs*	oh	*Crash!*
began	*The Old Dog*	open	*The Trunk of Money*
better	*Look at That Girl Go!*	park	*Crash!*
both	*The Car Wreck*	practice	*Sam and Dad*
bring	*Bees*	present	*Sick and Bored*
car	*Where Are the Keys?*	really	*The Scarecrow*
clothes	*I Want to Rest*	room	*What a Bike!*
cool	*What a Bike!*	saw	*Vote!*
couldn't	*Crash!*	school	*I Want to Rest*
covered	*The Toy Robot*	seen	*Not Mice!*
doctor	*Oh the Pain!*	shop	*Can You Come?*
done	*Sam Is the Best*	smiled	*The Trunk of Money*
don't	*Can You Come?*	someone	*Who Did It?*
door	*The Car Wreck*	soon	*The New Rug*
every	*Look at That Girl Go!*	suddenly	*The Car Wreck*
floor	*Stop That!*	talk	*The Toy Robot*
four	*Look at That Girl Go!*	though	*First Place*
friends	*I Want to Rest*	thought	*First Place*
hair	*Where Are the Keys?*	today	*The Car Wreck*
head	*Where Are the Keys?*	toward	*The Frog*
isn't	*Bob and the Bug*	under	*Where Are the Keys?*
jumped	*Oh the Pain!*	walk	*The Toy Robot*
key	*Where Are the Keys?*	wild	*The Clown*
laughed	*Bees*		

*Groupings based on the Fry Word List

Sight Words Routine: See, Hear, Write

CCSS.RF.K.3.C
TEKS 110.11.3.D

LEARNING OBJECTIVE: Read high-frequency, phonetically irregular words.
LANGUAGE OBJECTIVE: Identify and say high-frequency, phonetically irregular words.

Research

Developing readers need explicit instruction to automatically and accurately read irregular high-frequency words. Because these words are phonetically irregular, students must learn to recognize them on sight without sounding them out (Ehri, 2005; Wylie & Durrell, 1970).

Lesson Overview

Students learn and practice sight words by reading, hearing, saying, spelling, and writing target sight words.

Materials	Preparation
• Imagine Learning Sight Words List • Sight Word Flash Cards • Whiteboards	• Choose sight words from the Imagine Learning Sight Words List. • Cut out flash cards.

NOTE: Whiteboards can be made with pieces of cardstock inserted into plastic sheet protectors or three-ring binder covers.

Introduce the Activity: See, Hear, Write

NOTE: This example lesson uses *said* as the target sight word. For additional lessons, replace the target word and example sentence.

1. Introduce the concept Say: ***These are words you have seen recently in Imagine Learning stories. Practicing these words will help you read them when you see them again. These words are tricky and most can't be sounded out.***

2. Introduce individual sight word Display the flash card *said*. Say: ***This word is* said.** Sweep your finger under the word. ***What's the word?*** Sweep your finger under the word to signal student response. Have students repeat the word two more times as you sweep your finger under the word.

3. Use the word in a sentence Say: ***Now let's use it in a sentence: The teacher* said *to read a book. Say it with me.*** Repeat the sentence.

4. Spell the word Say: ***Look at this word and notice each letter as I spell it.*** Have students look at the word as you spell it aloud. Pause for one second between each letter. Have students spell the word chorally as you point to each letter. Call on a student to spell the word.

5. Write the word Distribute whiteboards. Display the flash card. Say: ***I want you to write* said *as big as you can on your board.*** Then have students write the word in all capital letters and as small as they can. Turn the flash card over and have students write the word without looking at the flash card.

6. Repeat Repeat the steps for each target sight word.

Check Progress

Observe each student during practice and use the following activity to check progress made on the target skill.

Show the flash card, say the word, and then turn the flash card over and have students write the word from memory.

If a student misspells a word, meet with him or her individually to review the misspelled word. Show the student the flash card and ask: ***What do you notice about the spelling of this word? What do you need to remember about this word to spell it correctly in the future?*** Prompt the student to try spelling the word again from memory.

Ehri, L.C. (2005). Learning to read words: Theory, findings, and issues. *Scientific Studies of Reading*, 9(2), 167–188.

Wylie, R.E., & Durrell, D.D. (1970). Teaching vowels through phonograms. *Elementary English*, 47, 787–791.

Sight Words Routine: Quick Recognition

CCSS.RF.K.3.C
TEKS 110.11.3.D

LEARNING OBJECTIVE: Read high-frequency, phonetically irregular words.
LANGUAGE OBJECTIVE: Recognize and read high-frequency, phonetically irregular words.

Research

Developing readers require multiple exposures to irregular high-frequency words. Irregular words should be practiced on a daily basis. Repeated practice with these words will help students recognize and read the words automatically (Bear et al., 2015; Carnine et al, 1997).

Lesson Overview

Students review sight words with the teacher and then read them from flash cards as quickly as possible.

Materials	Preparation
• Imagine Learning Sight Words List • 5–6 Sight Word Flash Cards	• Choose sight words from the Imagine Learning Sight Words List. • Cut out flash cards.

Introduce the Activity: Quick Recognition

NOTE: This example lesson uses *with* as the target sight word. For additional lessons, replace the target word.

1. Introduce the concept Say: ***These are words you have seen recently in Imagine Learning stories. These words can be tricky and most can't be sounded out. We're going to practice recognizing them quickly, so you don't get stuck when you are reading.***

2. Review sight words Review each of the words by pointing to a flash card, saying the word aloud, and having students repeat the word aloud. Display all words in random order on one line. Say: ***Let's read these words together.*** Starting with the word at the left and continuing to the right, point at each word and have the students read it aloud chorally. Then point to the words randomly and ask the students to read the word aloud.

3. Play Quick Recognition Gather the cards into a stack. Choose one student to start. Say: ***When I show you a word, read it aloud.*** Show the first card. If the student responds correctly within three seconds, say: ***Yes, the word is* with. *Say* with.** Have student repeat the word. Put the card in the middle of the deck. If the student responds incorrectly or hesitates for longer than three seconds, say: ***The word is* with. *Say* with.** Return the card to the middle of the deck. Repeat with new words, alternating through all students in the group.

Check Progress

Observe each student during practice and use the following activity to check progress made on the target skill.

When you have reviewed all of the flash cards in the stack at least once, shuffle the cards and meet with students individually to review them one more time. If a student has mastered each word, consider the intervention successful.

Bear, D.R., Invernizzi, M., Templeton, S., & Johnston, F. (2015). *Words their way* (6th ed.). Boston, MA: Pearson.

Carnine, D. W., Silbert, J., & Kameenui, E. J. (1997). *Direct instruction reading* (3rd ed.). Upper Saddle River, NJ: Merrill/Prentice-Hall.

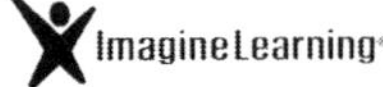

Sight Words Routine: Sight Word Games

CCSS.RF.K.3.C
TEKS 110.11.3.D

LEARNING OBJECTIVE: Read high-frequency, phonetically irregular words.
LANGUAGE OBJECTIVE: Recognize and read high-frequency, phonetically irregular words.

Research

Hands-on games and activities are effective in helping developing readers acquire and remember new information. Repeated exposure to irregular high-frequency words increases the probability of automatic identification by sight. Automatic recognition of irregular high-frequency words reduces the cognitive demands of reading and frees up cognitive capacity for other reading tasks (Bear et al., 2015; Ehri, 2005).

Lesson Overview

Teacher chooses from a variety of sight word games designed to help students practice reading sight words correctly.

POW!

Materials	Preparation
• Imagine Learning Sight Words List • 2 sets of Sight Word Flash Cards • POW! Cards • Timer	• Choose sight words from the Imagine Learning Sight Words List. • Cut out flash cards and POW! cards.

How to Play

1. Set up the game Mix both sets of flash cards and the POW! cards together and place the pile on a table or desk. Set a timer for one minute.

2. Play the game Instruct students to take turns selecting a card from the pile and quickly reading the word. If the students can read the word aloud correctly, they get to keep the card. If the students do not know the word, they give the card to the next person to read. If no one can read the word, set the card aside for review after the game. If a student selects a POW! card, he or she returns all of their cards to you. The student with the most cards at the end of one minute wins.

3. Review missed words At the end of the round, review any missed words. Practice reading the sight words and review what they mean.

EXTENSION ACTIVITY: Have students select one of their cards and make up a sentence for their word.

Check Progress

Observe each student during practice and use the following activity to check progress made on the target skill.

Use the Sight Word Flash Cards to quiz students. If the student is able to read the targeted sight words, consider the intervention successful.

Tic-Tac-Toe

Materials	Preparation
• Imagine Learning Sight Words List • 9 Sight Word Flash Cards (1 set per student pair) • 4 game markers for each student (matching buttons, coins, colored squares of paper)	• Choose sight words from the Imagine Learning Sight Words List. • Cut out flash cards.

How to Play

1. Set up the game Assign students to a partner. Instruct each partnership to take nine sight word cards and place them facedown in a 3 by 3 tic-tac-toe grid.

2. Play the game One partner turns over a card on the grid. If the student can read the word, he or she places his marker in that space. If the student can't read the word, then the he or she turns the card facedown. The other partner then takes a turn. The first player to get three in a row wins.

Check Progress

Observe each student during practice and use the following activity to check progress made on the target skill.

Use the Sight Word Flash Cards to quiz students. If the student is able to read the targeted sight words, consider the intervention successful.

Concentration

Materials	Preparation
• Imagine Learning Sight Words List • Sight Word Flash Cards (2 copies of same set per student pair)	• Choose sight words from the Imagine Learning Sight Words List. • Cut out flash cards.

How to Play

1. Set up the game Assign students to a partner. Give each partnership two sets of the same flash cards. Have students mix the flash cards together and lay them facedown on the table or desk.

2. Play the game Students take turns turning over two cards and reading each word out loud. If a student turns over a match and can read the word, he or she keeps the cards. If the words do not match or the student can't read the word, the student turns the cards facedown. If neither partner can read a word, they can ask for help. The student with the most matches at the end of the game wins.

Check Progress

Observe each student during practice and use the following activity to check progress made on the target skill.

Use the Sight Word Flash Cards to quiz students. If the student is able to read the targeted sight words, consider the intervention successful.

WORD-O

Materials	Preparation
• Imagine Learning Sight Words List • 9 or 16 Sight Word Flash Cards • Long or Short WORD-O Board (1 per student) • Game markers (buttons, coins, small pieces of paper)	• Choose 9 sight words (short version) or 16 sight words (long version) from the Imagine Learning Sight Words List. • Cut out flash cards.

How to Play

1. Set up the game Display the 9 or 16 flash cards you have selected. Have students copy each of the sight words into a space of the WORD-O board in random order. Each student should write words in different spaces. After students have written the words, shuffle the cards into a deck.

2. Play the game Call out a word from the deck. Have students use their markers to cover the word on their board. Repeat until a student covers up a whole row and calls out, "WORD-O!" Have the student read aloud each word in the row. If correct, he or she wins a point. Shuffle the deck and repeat the game.

Check Progress

Observe each student during practice and use the following activity to check progress made on the target skill.

Use the Sight Word Flash Cards to quiz students. If the student is able to read the targeted sight words, consider the intervention successful.

Bear, D.R., Invernizzi, M., Templeton, S., & Johnston, F. (2015). *Words their way* (6th ed.). Boston, MA: Pearson.

Ehri, L.C. (2005). Learning to read words: Theory, findings, and issues. *Scientific Studies of Reading*, 9(2), 167-188.

POW!

Reteaching Lessons

WORD-O

Long WORD-O Board

WORD-O

Reteaching Lessons

Sight Words Routine: Sight Word Soup

CCSS.RF.K.3.C
TEKS 110.11.3.D

LEARNING OBJECTIVE: Read high-frequency, phonetically irregular words.
LANGUAGE OBJECTIVE: Read and say high-frequency, phonetically irregular words.

Research

Many irregular high-frequency words are abstract, so developing readers need help looking carefully at high-frequency words as they commit them to memory. Repeated exposure builds automatic recognition of these irregular high-frequency words, which facilitates reading (Bear et al., 2015).

Lesson Overview

Students review sight words and read them as they make sight word soup.

Materials	Preparation
• Imagine Learning Sight Words List • 8–10 Sight Word Flash Cards • Bowl, bucket, or other container • Large spoon (optional) • Word Recognition Grids	• Choose sight words from the Imagine Learning Sight Words List. • Cut out flash cards. • Following the instructions in Check Progress, create Word Recognition Grids.

Introduce the Activity: Sight Word Soup

1. Introduce the concept Say: ***These are words you have seen recently in Imagine Learning stories. These words can be tricky and most can't be sounded out. We're going to practice recognizing them by making sight word soup. These words are our ingredients. Let's review them before we add them to the pot.***

2. Review sight words Read each word, use it in a sentence, then point out at least on characteristic of the word. For example, say: ***This is the word* are. *You* are *students. Ashley, this word begins with the same letter as your name.***

Possible word characteristics:

- This word begins with the same letter as your name
- This word has only three letters, just like the word *cat* that you learned yesterday
- All of the letters in this word have curves
- This word has two vowels
- This word has a smaller word inside it

3. Make sight word soup Have students repeat the spelling of the word after you. Say: ***Now I want you to say each letter in the word as I spell it aloud.*** Have the students spell the word aloud as you point to the letters. Then select one student, hand the student the card, and have the student read it aloud and drop it into the bowl. When all words have been added to the container, stir the cards around and announce that the sight word soup is ready. Have a student take a sight word out of the soup and read it aloud. Any words students cannot say quickly and correctly must be returned to the pot. Have students continue reading the words until all of the cards are removed from the pot.

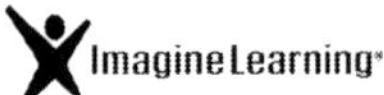

Check Progress

Observe each student during practice and use the following activity to check progress made on the target skill.

Create word recognition grids like the one shown here. Each horizontal row contains the same words in a different order. Create two grids to include all target sight words. Have each student read across one row on each grid. Point to each square in order, starting with the top row. If you have more students than rows, return to the top row. If the student can read each sight word in the row, consider the intervention successful.

from	said	your	was	this
your	from	this	said	was
was	this	from	your	said
said	your	was	this	from
this	was	said	from	your

Bear, D.R., Invernizzi, M., Templeton, S., & Johnston, F. (2015). *Words their way* (6th ed.). Boston, MA: Pearson.

a	and
are	as
be	but
by	can

do	for
from	have
he	his
I	is

it	not
of	one
or	said
she	that

the

their

there

they

this

to

was

we

were	what
which	with
you	your

about

been

come

could

down

first

get

go

has	her
him	into
like	look
make	many

more	my
no	now
number	other
out	people

Reteaching Lessons ✓

see	so
some	them
then	these
two	water

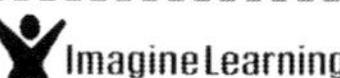

way

who

will

would

Reteaching Lessons

after	again
air	another
any	around
away	back

because

before

boy

does

even

found

give

good

Reteaching Lessons

here	house
know	me
mother	move
need	new

off	our
over	play
put	should
take	too

Reteaching Lessons

turn	us
very	want
where	work

across	afraid
against	always
baby	began
better	both

Reteaching Lessons

bring	car
clothes	cool
couldn't	covered
doctor	done

don't	door
every	floor
four	friends
hair	head

isn't	jumped
key	laughed
let's	money
moon	never

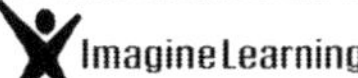

oh	open
park	practice
present	really
room	saw

Reteaching Lessons

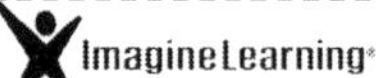

school	seen
shop	smiled
someone	soon
suddenly	talk

though	thought
today	toward
under	walk
wild	

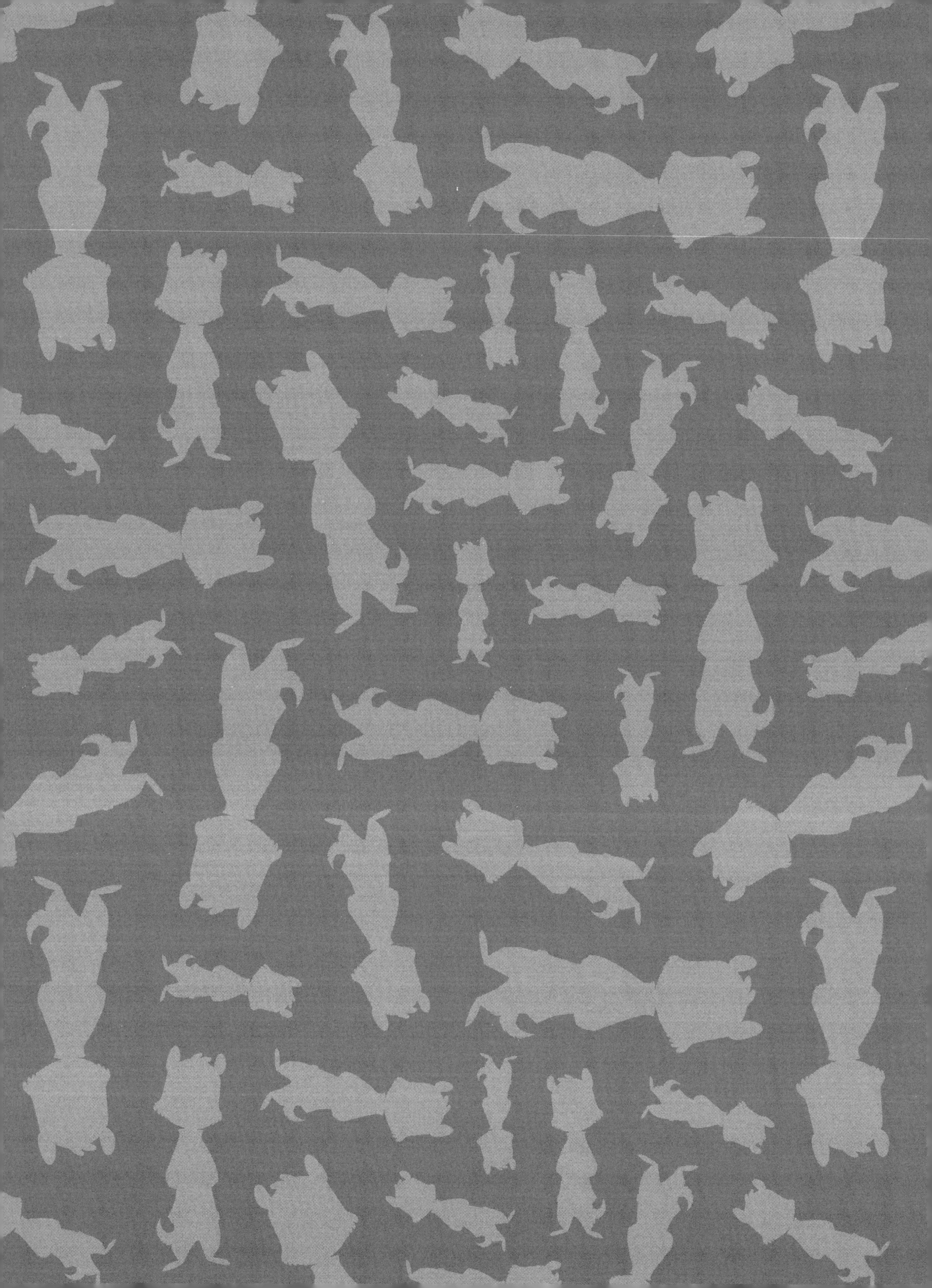

SPELLING

RETEACHING LESSONS

Developed with research-based methods, these instructional routines provide engaging activities and print-ready supporting materials to help reinforce spelling skills and build automaticity. Each spelling routine can be used for small group intervention and skill review or adapted for whole-class use. Also included in this section is a master list of spelling words from word families taught in the Imagine Learning online curriculum.

Analyze data in the Imagine Learning Action Areas Tool to identify groups of students who struggle with spelling, and use the Reteaching Lessons to provide additional support.

- Complete lesson plans that include modeling, practice, and assessment
- Lesson format that allows teachers to substitute easier or more challenging words, based on the individual needs of students
- Flexible grouping and suggestions for implementing differentiated instruction
- Materials and strategies specifically designed for struggling readers

Progress Tracking Sheet

Date	Student Name	Lesson/Skill	Intervention Successful (Y/N)	Notes

Progress Tracking Sheet

Date	Student Name	Lesson/Skill	Intervention Successful (Y/N)	Notes

Notes

Reteaching Lessons

Imagine Learning Spelling List

-ad	-ag	-am	-an	-ap	-at	-ack
bad	bag	dam	can	cap	bat	back
dad	rag	ham	fan	lap	cat	black
had	sag	jam	man	map	fat	crack
mad	tag	ram	ran	nap	hat	jack
pad	wag		tan	sap	mat	rack
sad			van	tap	sat	shack
				zap	vat	tack
						track

-and	-amp	-ash	-ace	-ake	-ame	-ane
band	camp	crash	brace	bake	blame	cane
bland	damp	dash	face	cake	came	lane
brand	lamp	flash	lace	fake	flame	mane
grand	ramp	lash	pace	make	frame	pane
hand		mash	place	take	game	
land		rash	race	rake	name	
sand		smash	space		same	
stand		trash	trace		shame	

-ate	-ail	-ain	-ay	-ed	-en	-et
crate	fail	drain	clay	bed	den	get
date	mail	main	day	fed	hen	jet
gate	nail	pain	gray	red	men	let
hate	pail	plain	lay	wed	pen	met
late	rail	rain	may		ten	set
skate	sail	train	play			wet
state			say			yet
rate			stay			
			way			

Reteaching Lessons

-ell	-end	-ent	-est	-eam	-eat	-eed
bell	bend	dent	best	beam	beat	feed
fell	mend	rent	chest	dream	cheat	deed
sell	send	sent	nest	gleam	cleat	need
smell	tend	tent	rest	ream	eat	reed
well		went	vest	seam	heat	seed
yell				steam	meat	
				team	seat	
					treat	
					wheat	

-eek	-eet	-id	-ig	-in	-ip	-it
cheek	beet	hid	big	bin	dip	fit
creek	feet	kid	dig	fin	lip	hit
peek	greet	lid	fig	pin	nip	kit
seek	meet	rid	pig	tin	rip	lit
week				win	sip	pit
					tip	sit
					zip	

-ick	-ill	-im	-ice	-ide	-ime	-ine
brick	drill	brim	mice	bride	chime	fine
flick	grill	dim	lice	glide	crime	line
kick	skill	him	nice	hide	dime	mine
lick	still	skim	price	pride	lime	nine
pick		slim	rice	ride	mime	shine
sick		swim		side	prime	
stick		trim		slime	slime	
thick				wide	time	

Reteaching Lessons

-ite	-ive	-ight	-ind	-y	-ob	-og
bite	dive	fight	bind	by	job	bog
kite	drive	light	find	cry	lob	dog
site	five	might	kind	dry	mob	fog
	hive	right	mind	fly	rob	jog
	live	sight		fry	sob	log
		tight		shy		blog
		bright		sky		clog
		flight		try		frog
		knight		why		smog
		fright				

-op	-ot	-ox	-ock	-omp	-op	-oke
bop	dot	box	block	chomp	crop	joke
cop	hot	cox	clock	romp	drop	poke
hop	lot	fox	dock	stomp	flop	woke
mop	not	pox	knock	tromp	shop	yoke
pop	pot		lock		stop	
top	tot		rock			
crop			shock			
drop			sock			
flop						
shop						
stop						

-one	-ope	-ote	-oat	-old	-ow	-ug
alone	cope	note	boat	cold	bow	bug
bone	hope	quote	coat	gold	blow	hug
cone	mope	tote	float	mold	corw	jug
lone	nope	vote	goat	old	flow	mug
phone	rope	wrote	moat	sold	grow	rug
prone	scope		oats	told	mow	tug
stone	slope				row	
tone					slow	
					snow	
					tow	

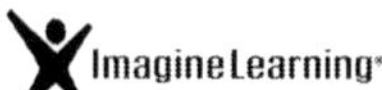

-um	-un	-ut	-uck	-ug	-ump	-ew
gum	bun	but	buck	slug	bump	blew
hum	fun	cut	duck	plug	jump	chew
sum	run	hut	luck	snug	pump	crew
yum	sun	nut	tuck	smug	lump	drew
		rut	stuck		dump	flew
			truck		plump	grew
			pluck		slump	stew
			snuck		clump	
					thump	

-ue	-all	-aw	-oud	-out	-ow	-own
blue	ball	jaw	cloud	about	bow	brown
clue	call	law	loud	out	brow	clown
cue	hall	paw	proud	pout	cow	crown
due	wall	raw	round	scout	how	down
glue	small	saw	sound	shout	now	frown
true	stall	claw		snout	pow	gown
argue		draw		trout	wow	town
issue		flaw				
value		straw				
		thaw				

-oi	-oy	-ool (long)	-oom (long)	-oon (long)	-oop (long)	-oot (long)
foil	boy	cool	boom	loon	coop	boot
oil	joy	fool	doom	moon	croop	hoot
soil	soy	pool	loom	noon	goop	loot
spoil	toy	tool	room	soon	hoop	scoot
	ahoy				loop	root
	decoy				scoop	
	enjoy				snoop	
	annoy				stoop	
					swoop	
					troop	

Reteaching Lessons

-ook (short)	-ood (short)	-ar	-ark	-irl	-irt	-ore
book	good	bar	bark	girl	dirt	bore
brook	hood	car	dark	twirl	flirt	chore
cook	stood	far	lark	swirl	shirt	core
crook	wood	jar	mark	whirl	skirt	more
hook			park			score
look			shark			shore
looks						snore
shook						sore
took						
unhook						

-orn	-ort	kn-	wr-	qu-	-ang	-ing
born	fort	knee	wrap	quit	bang	bring
corn	port	knit	wreck	quiz	fang	ding
horn	short	knob	wrist	quack	hang	king
thorn	snort	knot	write	quake	rang	ring
worn	sort	know	wring	queen	sang	sing
	sport	knead	wrong	quest		sting
		kneel	wrote	quick		swing
		knees		quiet		thing
		knife		quilt		
		knock		quote		

-ong	-ank	-ink	-unk
along	bank	blink	bunk
belong	blank	drink	chunck
gong	crank	ink	dunk
long	drank	pink	junk
song	sank	rink	skunk
strong	tank	sink	stunk
wrong	thank	stink	sunk
	yank	think	trunk
		wink	

Spelling Routine: Spelling Flip

CCSS.CCRA.L.2
TEKS 110.13.23.B

LEARNING OBJECTIVE: Spell grade-appropriate words correctly.
LANGUAGE OBJECTIVE: Correctly pronounce and spell grade-appropriate words.

Research

One of the key skills of successful spellers is the ability to recall visual images of words. Self-correction of spelling mistakes also enables students to find and notice spelling patterns they need to practice (Honig et al,. 2013).

Lesson Overview

Students use a flip folder to study each spelling word, practice spelling the word from memory, and check their spelling.

Materials	Preparation
• Printouts of Spelling Flip Folder Labels (one per student) • Spelling Flip Practice Sheet (one per student) • Manila file folder (one per student) • Student spelling list (one per student) • Imagine Learning Spelling List (optional)	• Create a flip folder for each student: 1. Glue the Spelling Flip Folder Labels to the front cover of a manila folder. 2. Open the manila folder and laminate it for repeated use. (optional) 3. Follow the dotted lines on the labels to cut the manila folder cover into thirds. 4. Insert a Spelling Flip Practice Sheet into each flip folder. 5. Create a student spelling list with 5–10 words from the Imagine Learning Spelling List. Display or make copies (one per student).

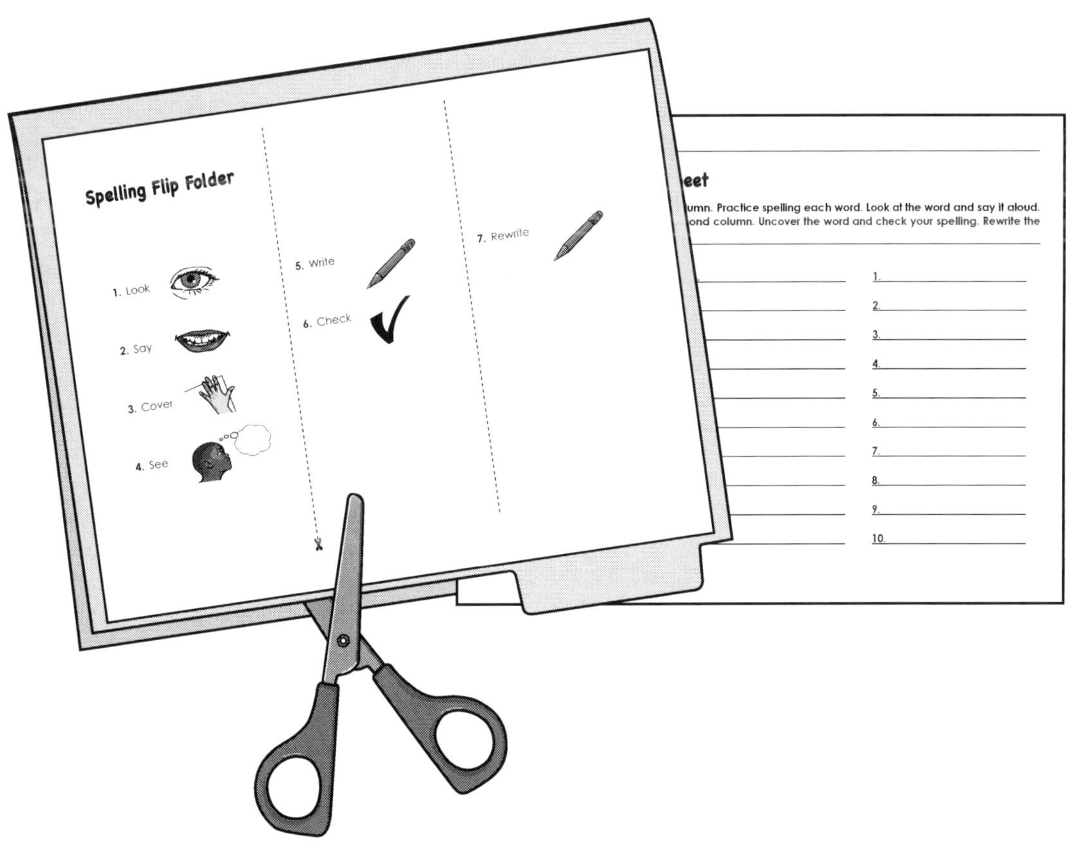

Introduce the Activity: Spelling Flip

Distribute or display the list of spelling words. Read each spelling word aloud and have the students read aloud each word after you.

Then distribute a Spelling Flip Folder to each student. Explain that students will use their flip folders to practice spelling words.

Have students copy each spelling word into the first column of their Spelling Flip Practice Sheets inside the flip folder.

Check to make sure students have correctly copied each word. Make corrections as necessary, or guide students to make corrections.

Then guide students to practice spelling the first word. Say:

1. ***Open the first flap and look at the first word.***
2. ***Say the word aloud.***
3. ***Close the flap to cover the word.***
4. ***See the word in your mind.***
5. ***Open the second flap. Write the word on the first blank line.***
6. ***Open the first flap to check the spelling. Close the second flap.***
7. ***Open the third flap and rewrite the word correctly.***

Have students continue in this manner to practice spelling the remaining words.

Check Progress

Check each student's Spelling Flip Practice Sheets and use the following activity to check progress.

Meet with students individually to review their Spelling Flip Practice Sheets. Together, look for a word the student has spelled incorrectly in the second column. Ask:

- ***When you checked your spelling of this word, what did you notice?***
- ***What do you need to remember about this word to spell it correctly in the future?***

Prompt students to try spelling the word again from memory.

Repeat with other words that were misspelled in the second column of the Spelling Flip Practice Sheet.

Honig, B., Diamond, L., & Gutlohn, L., (2013). *Teaching reading sourcebook* (2nd. ed.). Novato, CA: Arena Press.

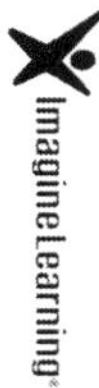

Spelling Flip Folder

1. Look 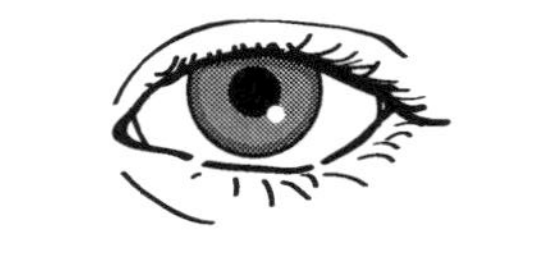

2. Say  

3. Cover 

4. See

5. Write 

6. Check 

7. Rewrite  

Name ______________________________

Spelling Flip Practice Sheet

Write the spelling words in the first column. Practice spelling each word. Look at the word and say it aloud. Cover the word and write it in the second column. Uncover the word and check your spelling. Rewrite the word in the third column.

1. ________	1. ________	1. ________
2. ________	2. ________	2. ________
3. ________	3. ________	3. ________
4. ________	4. ________	4. ________
5. ________	5. ________	5. ________
6. ________	6. ________	6. ________
7. ________	7. ________	7. ________
8. ________	8. ________	8. ________
9. ________	9. ________	9. ________
10. ________	10. ________	10. ________

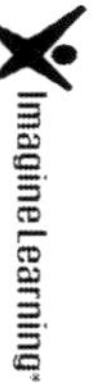

Spelling Routine: Word Sort

CCSS.CCRA.L.2
TEKS 110.13.23.B

LEARNING OBJECTIVE: Spell grade-appropriate words correctly.
LANGUAGE OBJECTIVE: Correctly pronounce and spell grade-appropriate words and explain sound-spelling patterns.

Research

Word-sorting activities require students to study the spelling and sound patterns in words. Research confirms that word sorts improve students' abilities to spell and read words (Bear et al., 2015; Honig et al., 2013). Using closed sorts, in which the teacher provides the categories, students begin to notice common spelling patterns. Speed sorts, in which students sort and write the words as quickly as possible, improve automaticity for writing and word attack skills.

Lesson Overview

Students sort spelling words into categories based on sound and spelling patterns.

Materials	Preparation
• Student spelling word list (one per student) • Word journals or notebooks (one per student; optional) • Clock with second hand or timers (for the Speed Sort) • Imagine Learning Spelling List (optional)	• Create student spelling word lists. Determine the number of word sort categories: 2, 3, or 4. For each category, select multiple words from the Imagine Learning Spelling List or your own classroom words. • Select one word for each category that you will use as your example words for modeling.

 NOTE: If students do not have a word journal already, they can create one using a notebook.

Introduce the Activity: Word Sort

1. **Introduce the Spelling Words** Distribute a student spelling word list to each student. Read each spelling word aloud and have students read aloud each word after you.
2. **Discuss Spelling Patterns** Say: ***Many words are similar because they have the same patterns of letters in them. Finding spelling patterns in words can help you learn how to be a better speller. You can sort words to help you remember the spelling patterns.***
3. **Model Sorting Words by Pattern** Display a blank sheet of paper and divide the paper into columns, one column per category. Introduce the categories and model sorting. For example, if you have chosen to do a two-category sort for *-ad* and *-ap*, draw one line down the center of the paper and label each column in the chart. Say: ***These are the spelling patterns you will look for today. This column is for words that have the letter pattern* -ad. *This column is for words that have the spelling pattern* -ap.**
   Then say: ***I will look at the first word on my spelling list and write the word in the column that has the same spelling pattern. If my first word is* dad, *I would write it below the letters* -ad.** Write *dad* under *-ad as you spell the word aloud, emphasizing the letters* -ad. ***If the next word is* tap, *where should I write it?*** (below the letters *-ap*) Write *tap* under *-ap.*
4. **Sort Words** Guide students to draw their own word sorting charts on paper or in their word journals. Have them label each section with the spelling patterns. Tell students to write each spelling word in the correct category on their word sort charts. See **Differentiation** suggestions.
5. **Share Word Sorts** Invite students to share one or two words from their completed word sort charts and describe the spelling patterns.

Differentiation
Below Level Guide the group to complete a shared word sort chart for the target spelling words. Add words to each category with input from students.
On Level Have students work with a partner to complete a shared word sort. Partners take turns writing a word in the correct category.
Above Level Call out each word to the students. Have them write the word in the correct category without looking at the spelling list.

Extension Activity: Speed Sort

To help students develop automaticity in writing spelling words, have them complete speed sorts. Have students sort the words again, this time writing the spelling words quickly and recording their time. Emphasize that the words must be spelled correctly and their writing must be legible. Students can repeat the speed sort, trying to beat their previous time.

> VARIATION: Guide students to sort spelling word cards instead of writing during the Speed Sort. Write the words on cards and show each card, one word at a time. Have students quickly identify the correct category for that word, responding orally or by pointing.

Check Progress

Observe each student during practice activities and use the following activity to check progress.

Use any of these prompts to quiz each student on two to three words from the list:

- ***Which spelling pattern does the word ___ have?***
- ***How are the words ____ and ____ alike?*** (for example: *map* and *tap*)
- ***Which of these words is spelled with the pattern ____?*** In random order, name one spelling word from the target category and two spelling words from other categories. For example, say: ***Which of these words is spelled with the pattern* -ack: band, camp, or crack?**

Bear, D., Invernizzi, M., Templeton, S., & Johnston, F. (2015). *Words their way* (6th ed.). Pearson Education.

Honig, B., Diamond, L., & Gutlohn, L., (2013). *Teaching reading sourcebook* (2nd ed.). Novato, CA: Arena Press.

Spelling Routine: Word Journals

CCSS.CCRA.L.2
TEKS 110.13.23.B

LEARNING OBJECTIVE: Spell grade-appropriate words correctly.
LANGUAGE OBJECTIVE: Correctly pronounce and spell grade-appropriate words in writing and relate them to their meaning.

Research

Word study notebooks provide students with regular opportunities to engage in word study using various techniques. Experts agree that word study should be active and engaging while providing regular opportunities for students to write the words and analyze their spelling patterns. Unlike rote learning, interacting creatively with spelling words using a multi-sensory approach helps to solidify long-term memory (Bear et al., 2015; Gentry et al., 1993; Honig et al., 2013).

Lesson Overview

Students use word journals in creative activities to write spelling words, study spelling patterns, draw pictures to show the words' meanings, and write the words in sentences to provide context.

Materials	Preparation
• Student spelling word list (one per student) • Word journals or notebooks (one per student)	• Review the Word Journal Activities chart and the Sample Word Journal Entries on the pages that follow. Select an activity for spelling word study. • Create student spelling word lists. Select words from the Imagine Learning Spelling List or your own classroom words. • Prepare context sentences for each of the target spelling words.

 NOTE: If students do not have a word journal already, they can create one using a notebook.

Introduce the Activity: Using Word Journals

1. **Introduce the Spelling Words** Distribute a student spelling word list to each student. Read each spelling word aloud and have students read aloud each word after you.
2. **Use Words in Context** Say the first spelling word in a sentence. Invite a volunteer to say the word in a sentence of their own. Continue with the remaining spelling words.
3. **Introduce the Word Journal Activity** Explain: ***Word journals can help you study spelling words in fun and creative ways. Here's an example of the word journal page you will make today.***
4. **Model the Activity** Show the example of the chosen journal activity and explain that students will create a similar entry in their own journals using spelling words from the list. Read aloud the directions in the Word Journal Activities chart.
5. **Create a Journal Entry** Distribute students' word journals if they don't already have them. Have students complete the assigned word journal activity, crossing off each spelling word from their list as they use the word in the journal. See **Differentiation** suggestions.
6. **Share Work** Invite students to share a drawing, sentence, or another part of their journal entries.

Differentiation
Below Level Guide the group to brainstorm ideas for the journal entry activity. Create a shared journal entry on a white board with input from students. Have students copy the shared journal entry into their own word journals.
On Level Have students work with a partner as they complete their journal entries. Partners should offer feedback to one another and check that their partner's words are spelled correctly.
Above Level Have students complete the word journal activity individually and then share what they've done with a partner.

Reteaching Lessons

Word Journal Activities	
Picture Dictionary	***For each spelling word on your list:*** ***1. Cover the word and write it from memory.*** ***2. Uncover the word and check the spelling.*** ***3. Draw a picture to show the word's meaning.*** ***4. Use the word to write a sentence under the picture.*** ***5. Underline the spelling word in your sentence.***
Write a Story	***1. Write a short story using as many spelling words as you can. Try writing the spelling words from memory.*** ***2. Underline each spelling word and check that they are spelled correctly.***
Create a Comic Strip	***Create a stick people comic strip using as many spelling words as you can.*** ***1. Draw stick people in each box and use spelling words to write captions or speech bubbles for each picture. Try writing the spelling words from memory.*** ***2. Underline the spelling words and check that they are spelled correctly.***
Word Ladders	***1. Write a spelling word from the list.*** ***2. Drop letters from the first word and add letters to create a new spelling word. You must keep at least two letters from the previous word.*** ***3. Underline the added letters in the new word.*** ***4. Continue with the next word. Create a word ladder with as many different spelling words as possible.***
Words in Color	***1. Write each spelling word.*** ***2. Check the spelling.*** ***3. Use crayons, colored pencils, or markers to rewrite each spelling word in color, or draw bubble letters and color them. Use one color for the consonants and a different color for the vowels.***

Check Progress

Check student word journal entries to make sure they have correctly spelled each target word and use the following activity to check progress.

Use prompts such as these to assess each student's knowledge of the spelling words:

- ***Were there any words that were hard to spell correctly without looking at your list?***
- ***What do you need to remember about that word next time?***

Prompt students to spell the problem word(s) again from memory.

Bear, D., Invernizzi, M., Templeton, S., & Johnston, F. (2015). *Words their way* (6th ed.). Pearson Education.

Gentry, J.R., Gillet, J.W. (1993). *Teaching kids to spell.* Portsmouth, NH: Heinemann.

Honig, B., Diamond, L., & Gutlohn, L. (2013). *Teaching reading sourcebook* (2nd ed.). Novato, CA: Arena Press.

Sample Word Journal Entries

My cat is soft.

Picture Dictionary

Clay likes to play on a gray day.
He runs in the rain.
He sets his train on a rail.
This is the way he has fun.

Write a Story

Reteaching Lessons

Sample Word Journal Entries

Create a Comic Strip

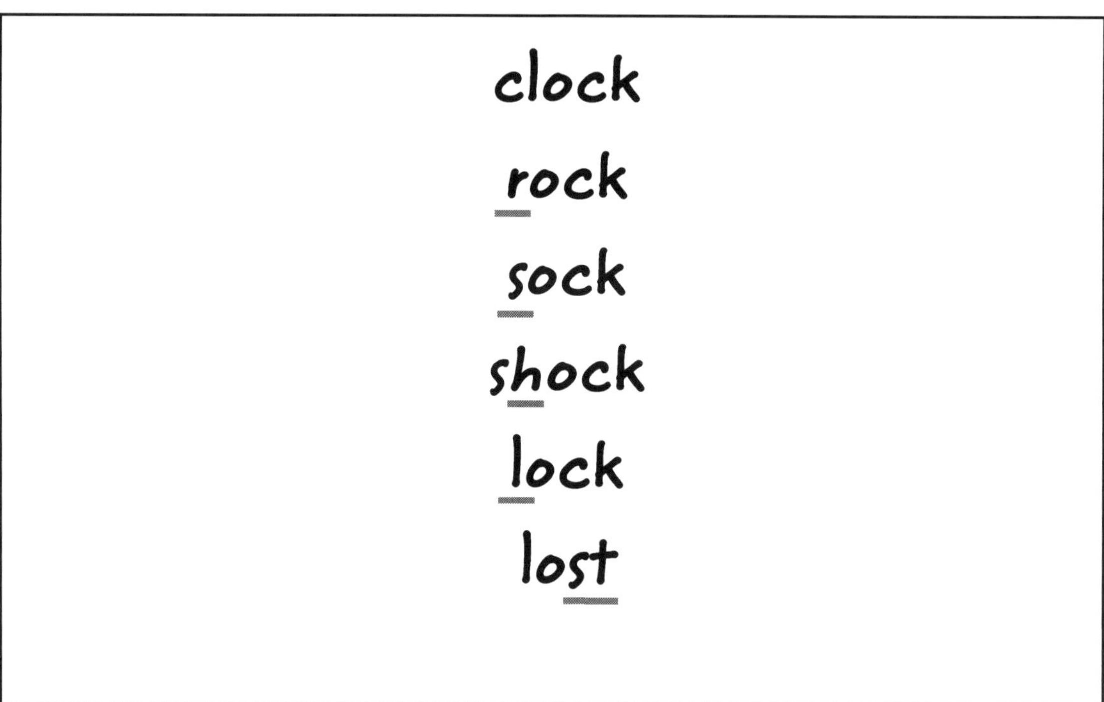

Word Ladders

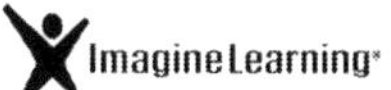

Sample Word Journal Entries

bake

cake

came

date

face

Words in Color

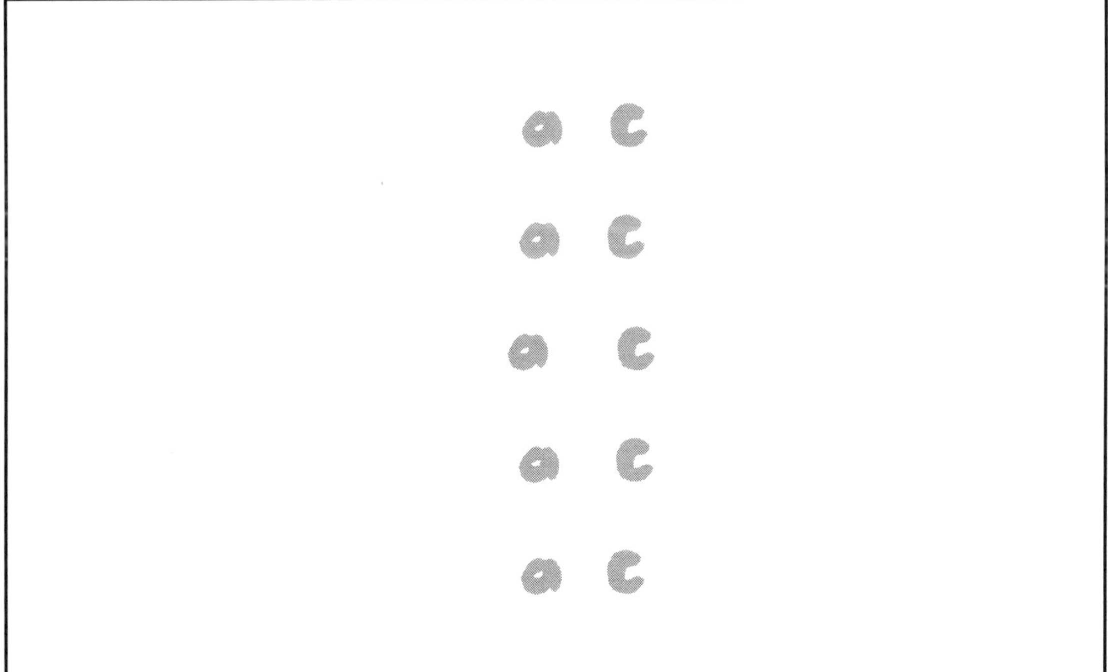

Words in Color

Spelling Routine: Spelling Games

CCSS.CCRA.L.2
TEKS 110.13.23.B

LEARNING OBJECTIVE: Spell grade-appropriate words correctly.
LANGUAGE OBJECTIVE: Correctly pronounce and spell grade-appropriate words orally and in writing.

Research

Research shows that spelling study is effective when students play games that are fun and engaging. Games that provide opportunities for students to analyze spelling patterns will improve students' reading as well as spelling (Bear et al., 2016; Beck et al., 2002). Games that require students to write words improve automaticity for writing and word attack skills (Honig et al., 2000).

Lesson Overview

Teacher chooses from a variety of spelling games designed to help students practice spelling words correctly, writing the words, and analyzing spelling patterns.

Tic-Tac-Toe

Materials	Preparation
• Index cards • Student spelling list (one per pair)	• Prepare student spelling lists. Select words from the Imagine Learning Spelling List or your own classroom words.

How to Play

1. **Identify Words for Practice** Distribute student spelling word lists. Assign each student a word for practice, or have students circle a word on the list that they want to practice spelling. Have students write their assigned word on an index card or piece of paper and compare it to the word list to make sure it is spelled correctly.
2. **Pair Students** Assign students to a partner to play the game. Have each student give the index card with their word to their partner.
3. **Play the Game** Have pairs of students start by drawing a tic-tac-toe board. The first player writes his or her assigned spelling word in a space. The other player uses the index card to verify that it is spelled correctly, then writes his or her spelling word in another space.

   The players take turns, each writing his or her word in different spaces and checking their partner's words. If a player spells a word incorrectly, the partner can erase it and write his or her own word in that space.

   Players continue taking turns until one player has three spelling words in a row or the board is full. Students then choose new words and play a new round.

Check Progress

Use the following activity to check progress.

Collect the index cards from each student and quiz them on their assigned words. Say the spelling words and have students write them or spell them aloud.

Concentration

Materials	Preparation
• Index cards • Student spelling list (one per pair)	• Prepare student spelling lists. Select words from the Imagine Learning Spelling List or your own classroom words.

How to Play

1. **Pair Students** Assign students to a partner to play the game.
2. **Create Spelling Word Cards** Have partners create spelling word cards. Each student in the pair writes each spelling word on a different card. Tell students to compare their cards to the word list to make sure each word is spelled correctly.
3. **Students Shuffle the Cards** Have partners shuffle their cards together and lay them face down in a grid.
4. **Play the Game** Students take turns turning over two cards and reading them aloud. If the player turns over two matching cards, he or she spells the word aloud without looking at the cards. If the player correctly spells the word, he or she keeps the two cards. If the player misspells the words, he or she turns the cards facedown again and the turns ends. The player with the most cards in the end wins the game.

   VARIATION: If time is limited, allow students to turn over three cards on each turn, if two of the cards match, and the player can spell the word, he or she keeps the matching cards and turns the third back over.

Check Progress

Use the following activity to check progress.

Draw a card at random from the student's stack and say the word. Have the student spell the word aloud.

Daisy

Materials	Preparation
• Index cards • Spelling list	• Prepare a spelling word list that can be displayed to the group. Select words from the Imagine Learning Spelling List or your own classroom words.

How to Play

1. **Display the Spelling Words** Display the list of spelling words for students.
2. **Play a Group Game** Draw blank lines to represent each letter of a spelling word. For example, if the word is plane, draw five lines: __ __ __ __ __ . Have students take turns guessing a letter in the word. If the letter is in the word, write it in the corresponding blank. If the letter guess is not in the word, draw a circle to represent the center of a daisy. For the next incorrect letter, draw a daisy petal. The goal is for the students to guess all the letters in the spelling word before you draw a complete daisy with five petals, a stem, and two leaves.

   VARIATION: Pair students with a partner. Have pairs play the game with other spelling words.

Check Progress

Use the following activity to check progress.

Remove the displayed spelling list. Draw blank lines to represent a spelling word. Say the word and call on a student to write each letter of the words on the blanks. Continue until each student has had two turns.

Reteaching Lessons

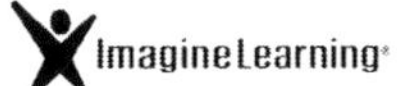

What's the Word?

Materials	Preparation
• Index cards • Spelling word list with ten words (two copies)	• Create word clue cards by writing five of the ten spelling words, each on a different index card. Then list three or four clues about each word's spelling. Plan clues so that by the final clue, students can narrow down the choice to one word. See the Sample Word Clue Card and step 3.

How to Play

1. **Assign Teams** Divide the group into two teams. Have each team place a spelling word list where all members of the team can see it.
2. **Review Spelling Words and Create Lists** Have each team create four additional copies of the spelling word list. Check that each word on their lists is spelled correctly.
3. **Give a Clue** Have each team use one shared list for each spelling word clue card. Read aloud the first clue on one of the word cards. Tell students to narrow down the possible spelling word by crossing off words that don't match the clue. Continue with the remaining clues until there is only one possible choice.
4. **What's the Word?** Have each team secretly write the correct word on a piece of paper. Invite teams to display their answers. Teams score one point if they answer correctly.
5. **Continue the Game** Continue with the remaining four word clue cards and student word lists.

LATE
The word contains the letter t.
The word has four letters.
The word will finish this sentence:
I was two minutes ____.

Sample Word Clue Card

Check Progress

Use the following activity to check progress.

Read the first clue from a clue card. Have each student write at least one spelling word from the list that matches the clue. Call volunteers to say and spell their word aloud. Repeat until each student has identified and spelled two words.

Word Scramble

Materials	Preparation
• Index cards • Spelling list	• Prepare a spelling list that can be displayed to the group. Select words from the Imagine Learning Spelling List or your own classroom words.

How to Play

1. **Display the Spelling Words** Display the list of spelling words for students.
2. **Scramble a Word** Secretly choose a spelling word from the list. Then slowly call out each letter of the word in random order as students write the letters.
3. **Unscramble the Word** Have students unscramble the word, write it out with the correct spelling, and raise their hand. The first student to unscramble the word correctly gets a point.
4. **Continue the Game** Continue the game with other words on the list.

Check Progress

Use the following activity to check progress.

Remove the displayed spelling list. Say three to four spelling words and have students write the words. Check their papers. If students can correctly spell the words, consider the intervention successful.

Bear, D., Invernizzi, M., Templeton, S., & Johnston, F. (2016). *Words their way* (6th ed.). Pearson Education.

Beck, I. L., McKeown, M.G., & Kucan, L., (2002). *Bringing words to life*. New York: Guilford.

Honig, B., Diamond, L., & Gutlohn, L., (2000). *Teaching reading sourcebook* (2nd ed.). Novato, CA: Arena Press.

Spelling

Spelling Routine: Frog Hop

CCSS.CCRA.L.2
TEKS 110.13.23.B

LEARNING OBJECTIVE: Spell grade-appropriate words correctly.
LANGUAGE OBJECTIVE: Correctly pronounce and spell grade-appropriate words and use them in spoken sentences.

Research

Spelling games give students the opportunity to actively engage while studying spelling words and patterns. Self-correction of spelling mistakes also enables students to find and notice spelling patterns they need to practice (Bear et al., 2016; Honig et al., 2000).

Lesson Overview

Students play a spelling board game that requires them to spell the words aloud and use them in sentences.

Materials	Preparation
• Index cards • Frog Hop Spelling Game Board (one per student pair) • Board game place markers (cut from game board) • Number cubes (one per student pair) • Imagine Learning Spelling List (optional)	• Use the index cards to make a set of 5–10 spelling word cards for each student. Alternatively, have the students prepare their own set of cards from a list before beginning the game. Each student may be assigned a different set of spelling words.

 NOTE: Frog Hop Spelling is best used as a review of previously studied spelling words.

Introduce the Activity: Play a Board Game

1. **Review the Spelling Words** Distribute each set of spelling word cards to students. Invite each student to read his or her spelling word cards aloud.
2. **Introduce the Game** Display a copy of the Frog Hop Spelling game board. Explain: ***You and a partner will play a board game to practice spelling words. Before you begin, you will exchange cards with your partner so you can quiz each other on your assigned spelling words and race to the end of the lily pad path.***
3. **Read the Directions** Read aloud the directions from the Frog Hop Spelling game board. Tell students: ***As you play the game, write a checkmark on your partner's word card every time he or she spells the word correctly. Write a question mark each time your partner misspells the word. Then put the card on the bottom of their stack.***
4. **Model the Game** Place two markers on the game board and invite a volunteer to model the game with you. Be sure to show students how to leap over a space occupied by another player.
5. **Play the Game** Assign students to a partner. Then distribute a copy of the Frog Hop Spelling game board, one number cube, and two frog markers to each pair. Have partners exchange spelling word cards and play the game.

   VARIATION**:** Have students use the word in a sentence to earn an extra turn.

Reteaching Lessons

Check Progress

Meet with students individually or in pairs to check their spelling word cards. Use the following activity to check progress.

Look through the student's stack of cards for question marks. If the student has no words with questions marks, randomly choose at least two words. Use any of these prompts quiz the student on those words:

- ***Read this word aloud.***
- ***Look at this word. Then cover it up and try spelling it.***
- ***I'll say the word and you spell it aloud.***
- ***What do you need to remember about this word to spell it correctly in the future?***

If students can correctly spell each word, consider the intervention successful.

Bear, D., Invernizzi, M., Templeton, & S., Johnston, F. (2016). *Words their way* (6th ed.). Pearson Education.

Honig, B., Diamond, L., & Gutlohn, L., (2000). *Teaching reading sourcebook* (2nd ed.). Novato, CA: Arena Press.

Frog Hop Spelling

Cut off corner along solid line. Fold on dotted lines to create a standing frog game board marker.

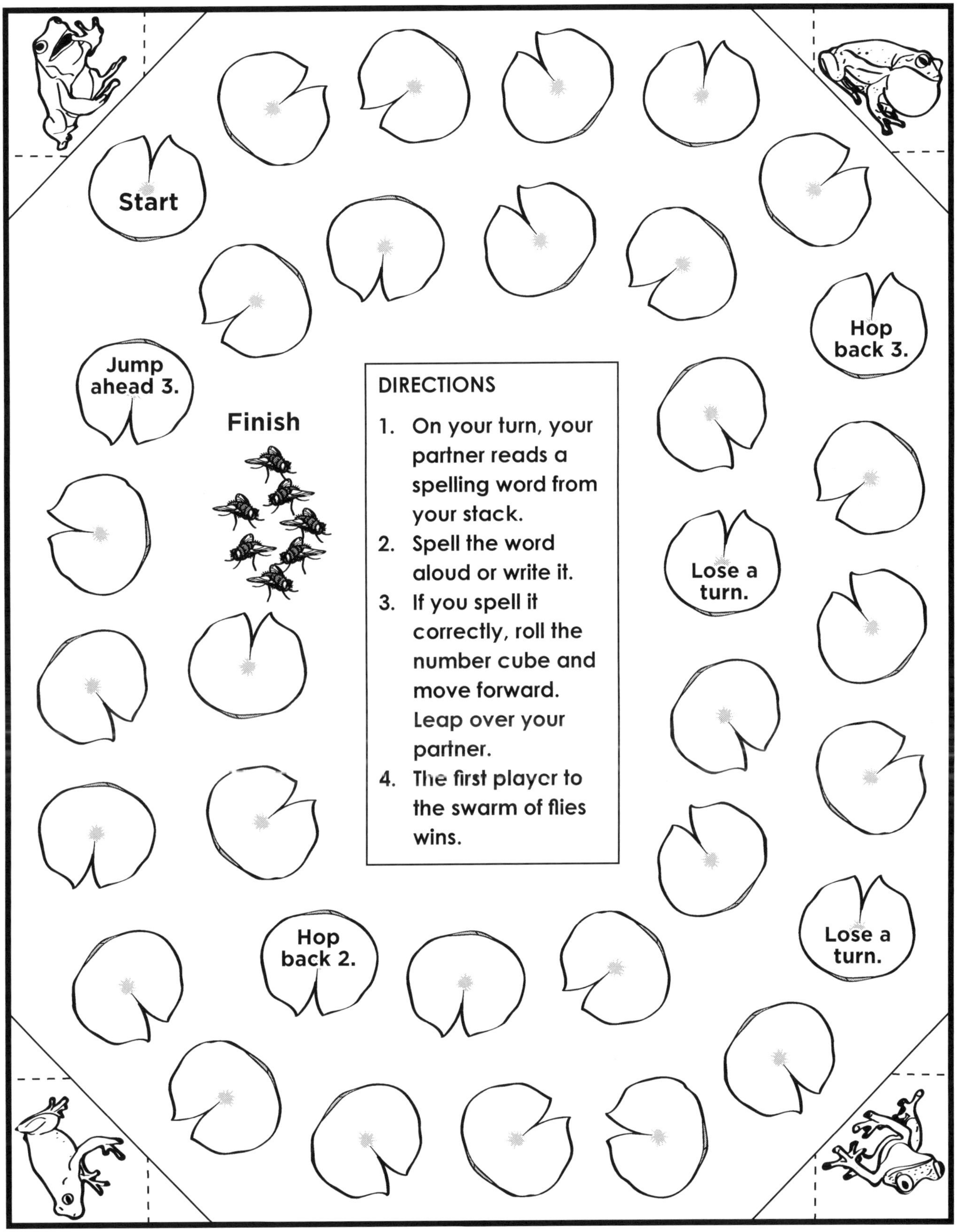

Start

Jump ahead 3.

Finish

Hop back 3.

Lose a turn.

Hop back 2.

Lose a turn.

DIRECTIONS

1. On your turn, your partner reads a spelling word from your stack.
2. Spell the word aloud or write it.
3. If you spell it correctly, roll the number cube and move forward. Leap over your partner.
4. The first player to the swarm of flies wins.

Reteaching Lessons

Made in the USA
San Bernardino, CA
09 February 2017